28298

28298

THE SCRIPT OF
HUMANISM

JAMES WARDROP

THE SCRIPT OF HUMANISM

Some Aspects of

Humanistic Script

1460—1560

OXFORD

At the Clarendon Press

1963

Oxford University Press, Amen House, London E.C.4

GLASGOW NEW YORK TORONTO MELBOURNE WELLINGTON
BOMBAY CALCUTTA MADRAS KARACHI LAHORE DACCA
CAPE TOWN SALISBURY NAIROBI IBADAN ACCRA
KUALA LUMPUR HONG KONG

PRINTED IN GREAT BRITAIN
AT THE UNIVERSITY PRESS, OXFORD
BY VIVIAN RIDLER
PRINTER TO THE UNIVERSITY

PREFATORY NOTE

Aт the time of the author's death in 1957 the manuscript of this book was not in its final state of preparation. The footnotes and the scheme for the illustrations were incomplete and the author would doubtless have given the text a final revision. It is known that he intended to incorporate in this study the results of his later research, particularly in relation to Bartolomeo Sanvito. In editing the manuscript no attempt has been made to insert footnotes where it is known that they were lacking, and the bibliography does not include works which have appeared since 1953 when the lectures were delivered. It is probable that the author intended to use more illustrations than are reproduced here, but in the absence of precise indications it seemed better to confine them for the most part to the manuscripts cited in the text.

In the task of preparing the book for publication I have received much help from my father's former colleagues at the Victoria and Albert Museum and have relied on the advice and unfailing assistance of Professor Carlo Dionisotti.

E. M. W.

CONTENTS

LIST OF PLATES

INTRODUCTION

When the following pages were written there was no design to print them. Under the title 'Some aspects of humanistic script, 1460–1560', they were delivered in March 1952 to advanced students of palaeography at King's College, Strand, as the annual course of special lectures in that subject, sponsored by the University of London. Renaissance palaeography is rarely treated in academic instruction: the theme was new to most of the students I addressed; and I conceived it appropriate to sketch a background; to indicate certain principles; to suggest a point of view, rather than to conduct, *literatim*, a commentary on the slides, such as my audience might have had reason to expect. The point of view—that scripts are not to be studied in isolation; and that it is at least admissible to consider them as the products of human intelligence and skill—has, it seems, found some favour within and beyond the University. Deferring to the instances of friends, I have used the permission of London University, and the facilities granted me by the Clarendon Press, to make my observations public. The occasion has been taken to furnish the lectures with an apparatus, bibliographical and critical, which gives them a firmer basis, and may increase their usefulness. At the same time the illustrations have been augmented; here and there, by substitution, improved. For the sake of brevity the title has been changed; a departure justified also by the retrospect beyond 1460, which it was thought expedient to take, as an introduction. No attempt has been made to alter the structure of the text: I have not scrupled to retain what a candid critic was pleased to call my 'irrelevancies'; and, excepting a few minor modifications, it is here given as it was spoken.

So much by way of premise. There remains the most exacting task of all: to proffer the acknowledgements which a grateful duty prompts, and convention requires. Studies, conducted in solitude, grow by commutation and congress. When an author would recall and enregister the names of those 'but for whom', as the common formula runs, 'this book would never have been written' he must embrace, however slight his book, an ever-widening, ever-receding circle of friendship and professional acquaintance. Where is he to begin? I for one in times when the peculiar bent of my studies was not as yet imagined or defined. Thus, to the poet Raúl Jaimes Freyre, whose company I enjoyed almost daily throughout the course of two distant but impressionable years, I would inscribe words which he, grown old on the other side of the Andes, is never likely to read. He was my first contact with a living latin culture, derived in unbroken succession from Lucan and Quintilian and Martial; and from him I learned, before I knew a syllable of Tuscan, to lisp the 'habla rudo y grave del castellano'. Next, to Gilbert Highet in America, to whom I promised a book, I make this shadowy token, for the friendship of twenty-five years, and the stimulus of his conversation, his letters and his books. To Monsignor Enrico Carusi, late of the Vatican Library, my first sponsor and cicerone there, my thanks which should have been copious are now unavailing: what follows is an implied tribute to his memory.

The extent of my obligation to colleagues in the British Museum and Bodleian Libraries is best known to themselves, in terms of the trouble they have taken on my account, and of which none has ever complained. In the former, my demands have borne most heavily upon Mr. A. F. Johnson, Mr. T. C. Skeat, Dr. C. E. Wright, Mr. A. Mayor, and Mr. T. J. Brown; in the latter, on Dr. R. W. Hunt. I owe a special debt of gratitude to those private owners who have from time to time made available the manuscripts in their possession: to the Duke of Wellington, the Duke of Devonshire, and the Earl of Leicester; to Sir Sidney C. Cockerell, Dr. Eric Millar, Mr. Harvey Frost, Mr. A. Cherry-Garrard, Mr. Philip Hofer, and the Librarian of Brompton Oratory. My thanks are also due to the following institutions: to the Bodleian Library, Oxford, Cambridge University Library, King's College, Cambridge, Leeds University, Eton College; in Rome to the Vatican Library where I have enjoyed the assistance and collaboration of Dr. Augusto Campana; also in Rome to the Biblioteca Nazionale Vittorio Emanuele II, the Archivio di Stato, and the Biblioteca Casanatense; in Milan to the Biblioteca Ambrosiana; in Padua to the Museo Civico and the Archivio di Stato; in Venice to the Biblioteca Marciana, the Archivio di Stato, and the Museo Correr; and in Florence to the Biblioteca Medicea Laurenziana and the Biblioteca Nazionale Centrale; and in Amsterdam to the University Library.

The Rise of Humanistic Cursive: Antiquarian and Scholarly Influences

Even in this the sixth decade of our century the subject of humanistic script might seem to require at least a preliminary word of explanation or apology. Taking the wide view of palaeography, there is in theory no reason why its operation, unlike that of any other science, should be finite and terminable; and I have in fact presumed the operation of palaeography to be valid for as long as books continue to be written by hand. Perhaps in that I have been over-sanguine; for though there are signs that the exclusive view is beginning to be modified, there is still, I imagine, a disposition on the part of many palaeographers to regard post-medieval scripts—if these indeed are allowed to have any *locus standi* at all—as lying somehow beyond the confines of the faculty, in a sort of no-man's-land betwixt the desert and the sown, where a few perfervid italianates, a scattering of typographers, and some amateurs of fine writing may potter pathetically at their will.

A witness to the reality of this situation is the paucity of literature—of serious and informed literature—on the subject.[1] True, the aesthetics of humanistic writing—or rather of one belated and on the whole decadent aftergrowth of humanistic writing—have been widely canvassed; but aesthetics, it would appear, were a secondary consideration, at least with the fathers of humanism; and despite the emergence here and there of certain conspicuous landmarks (landmarks to which I shall presently refer) we are still a long way from possessing a full and accurate delineation, an ordnance survey map as it were, of the palaeographical tract lying between the death of Petrarch in 1374 and, say, the Sack of Rome in 1527.[2] It will be part of the purpose of this study, first to suggest that such a survey (exceeding, as in its complexity it must exceed, the capacity of any one scholar, or maybe of any one generation of scholars) ought to be made; secondly to indicate

---

[1] But see *infra*, pp. 5–6.

[2] An outline of the situation has been sketched by D. Thomas, 'What is the origin of the *Scrittura umanistica*?', in *Bibliofilia*, liii, Firenze, 1951, pp. 1–10.

something of what has already been done and what there remains to do; and thirdly to submit that the doing of it is a task which might properly and profitably engage the attention of advanced students of palaeography.

If, on the other hand, we hold to the literal and isolationist view of palaeography, that it is the science or art of deciphering, and determining the date of, ancient manuscripts[1]—that and nothing more—then we must be prepared, following Maunde Thompson,[2] to abandon the pursuit of the latin minuscule as soon as we reach the fifteenth century; or, having condescended to look into a humanistic codex and having found that, in the words of Steffens, *der Text bietet keine Schwierigkeit*,[3] we shall be justified in closing the book and bestowing our attentions elsewhere. Certainly, whatever else may be said of humanistic scripts, they are seldom difficult to read: our formal conventions and our standard of legibility in type derive directly from them, and the family resemblance is disarming: contractions are absent or few or easy of resolution, factors sufficient in themselves to diminish curiosity, if not altogether to suppress it. But, as every advanced student of the subject knows, palaeography imposes other obligations— some of them obvious, some less so—than those of decipherment and dating. The palaeographer must take into account the evolutionary processes of which scripts have been patient; he must know how scripts, in the words of an eminent American stylist, 'got that way'; and the better palaeographer he is, the more will he be aware that scripts 'got that way' not from any prepotency in themselves, but because of the purpose underlying them; because (to reduce it to its simplest terms) people and things, in all ages, were set against a specific intellectual, social, and economic background; because men pursued this or that ideal, or illusion, or appetite, and made or unmade themselves in the process. Thence the student may be led to the conclusion —a trite enough conclusion, but one often missed—that the ultimate value of palaeography, as indeed of any humane study whatsoever, lies in just what it has to tell us about people and things.

Assuming the assent of my reader to that general proposition, I may be permitted to dispense, once for all, with special pleading. Considered in terms of human behaviour, it follows of course that any study which brings

---

[1] *O.E.D.*
[2] *An Introduction to Greek and Latin Palaeography*, Oxford, 1912, p. 472.
[3] *Lateinische Paläographie*, Freiburg, 1903, p. 93.

us face to face with the histories, the passions, and the artefacts of the Italian Renaissance opens up a field fertile in every rich and vital qualification. To say that is not to impugn the humane values of the Middle Age. But the medieval manuscript tradition is for the most part anonymous: it is rarely, except by hearsay or inference, that we know by whom, or for whom, or even in what cloister a medieval manuscript was written. With Renaissance manuscripts we emerge from the cloister to the secular highway; we are among human documents, in the closest sense of that overworked term; we mingle at almost every turn with known personalities, with those who created a new organ for the human spirit; and who, as the founders of modern thought, released energies which still control the intellectual mechanism of the civilized world. Hence we may confidently expect the personalities and the scripts of the humanists mutually to illustrate and explain one another; and in our study of the latter, we shall succeed in proportion as we come close to the intention of the humanists themselves.

If we attend to the beginnings of humanism in Florence at the close of the fourteenth century and in the opening decades of the fifteenth,[1] we shall see it as an essentially literary movement inspired by the example of Francesco Petrarca;[2] and its progenitors—Coluccio Salutati,[3] Niccolò Niccoli,[4] Poggio Bracciolini[5]—as a group of scholars engaged in an act not so much of creation as of recovery:[6] men, in short, with the wit to take first things first. A treasure, the literary heritage of ancient Rome, had been lost or laid aside; it was for them, the early humanists, to restore the treasure; for their successors, if they were so minded, to invest it, and on the product to build

---

[1] To seek the origins of humanism in remoter times, and in places other than Florence, is the tendency of modern criticism. See, for example, G. Billanovich, 'Petrarch and the textual tradition of Livy', in *Journal of the Warburg and Courtauld Institutes*, xiv. 3–4, London, 1951, pp. 137–208, esp. p. 208; idem. *I Primi Umanistici e le Tradizioni dei Classici Latini*, Fribourg (Switzerland), 1953.

[2] (1304–74). For the bibliography of Petrarch see *Enciclopedia Italiana*. Cf. especially P. de Nolhac, *Pétrarque et l'humanisme*, 2nd ed., Paris, 1907, on which a conspicuous advance has been made by the current studies of Billanovich (*ut supra*). See also his *Petrarca letterato, I, Lo scrittoio de Petrarca*, Roma, 1947.

[3] (1331–1406). See F. Novati, *Epistolario di Coluccio Salutati*, Roma, 1891–1911; A. v. Martin, *Coluccio Salutati und das humanistische Lebensideal*, Leipzig, 1916. The definitive work on Salutati, by B. L. Ullman, is in progress.

[4] (1363–1437). See G. Zippel, *Niccolò Niccoli, contributo alla storia dell'umanesimo*, &c., Firenze, 1890; idem. in *Giornale storico della letteratura italiana*, xxiv, Torino, 1894, pp. 166–86.

[5] (1380–1459). See E. Walser, *Poggius Florentinus*, Leipzig, 1914.

[6] See G. Voigt, *Il risorgimento dell'antichità classica, ovvero il primo secolo dell'umanesimo*, Firenze, 1888–97; R. Sabbadini, *Le scoperte dei codici latini e greci nei sec. XIV e XV*, Firenze, 1905; A. C. Clark, 'The reappearance of the texts of the classics', in *The Library*, 4th ser., ii, London, 1922, pp. 13–42.

the Palace of Art. Here it is most important that the student should be cautioned against reading into the infancy of the Renaissance, elements which, if present at all, were characteristic rather of its maturity. To the early humanists that which mattered most was antiquity—antiquity first and foremost: antiquity for its own sake. Antiquity was the sovereign authority to which, at all seasons and in all things, they instinctively referred. Their attitude to it was corporate, almost anonymous. The intense individualism which throws into such dazzling relief the character of an Alberti, a Leonardo, or even, later still, a Cellini, was scarcely theirs. In the crises and conjunctures of life the question which the humanists would ask themselves was not, as Alberti or Leonardo or Cellini would have done, how, in this or that situation, can I most be myself; what can I extract from it in point of self-realization; but how, in the given circumstances, would an ancient Roman or Greek have behaved.

Many people make the mistake of regarding the humanist scribal reform as a battle waged by Roman against Goth, just as a later declared conflict has been imagined between printer and scribe. Thence it is an easy step into the equally dangerous error of interpreting the whole humanist movement as a revolt, or a series of revolts. That general heresy we have not here the time to examine or refute. What it should interest us to remember is, that when the first humanists, intent on the reduplication of the new-found texts of the classics, chose as the vehicle of their transcription the carolingian minuscule in which those texts themselves were written, the humanists made that choice not so much because the carolingian minuscule was beautiful, as because it was old. That it was also, incidentally, expeditious and clear, was a latin quality in which they must equally have rejoiced. Just how old the humanists judged the carolingian minuscule to be is another question. It is scarcely to be supposed that Niccolò Niccoli or Poggio believed the St. Gall manuscripts to have been written by the contemporaries of Cicero; but at any rate those lay closest to the classical world whose spirit they were so zealously bent on resurrecting, and the script was for that reason venerable and good. It was also in the highest degree appropriate.

Thus it happens that the revived caroline, which to our eyes, prepossessed with typographical standards, looks modern, was by the humanists called, not *littera formosa* or *lettera bella*, but *lettera antica*—the old writing.[1] It was

---

[1] *Lettera moderna* was, *per contra*, a gothic script.

not therefore in essence an aesthetic revulsion which caused them to discard
the gothic scripts which the revived caroline supplanted. If it had been so the
reform might have made little headway. No tradition is broken or impaired
merely by saying that you do not like it. It may be modified by demon-
strating its inappropriateness to some manifestly great purpose you have in
hand: this the humanists did. The gothic tradition in writing had, as we well
know, many years of lively existence before it; and no humanist would
have questioned the use of gothic script in a vernacular text. Nor was it ever
a solecism to indite modern latin verses in gothic. As late as the pontificate
of Leo X, it was thought a graceful compliment to him, when the exquisite
neo-classical poet, Marcantonio Casanova,[1] lost in the Sack of Rome, presented to the Pope the manuscript of his 'Heroica' now in Naples, written
in *bollatica*;[2] and a generation later Fausto Sabeo, custodian of the Vatican
Library,[3] made with commendation a similar gift to an equally exalted and
exacting patron, Francis the First.[4] But the substance of Petrarch's judgement stands; and it may be taken to epitomize, as it anticipates, the view
of his immediate successors: for the artist, gothic if you will; for the scholar,
something *castigata et clara*.[5]

I have not scrupled to use the terms 'gothic', 'roman', 'italic', and so on.
They may be bad palaeography, but they are good currency; and they have
the advantage of summoning to mind an unambiguous if imprecise image.
I have therefore retained these terms, believing that it would be sometimes
inconvenient to substitute, even if it were easy to propose, others that would
be unexceptionable.

As a beginning, the advanced student would do well to seek out, in the
British Museum Catalogue, anything listed under the name of Nicola
Barone,[6] and to use with discretion what he finds. For all practical purposes the first serious investigation, in English, of the scripts of humanism
with reference to the autographs of its founders, was made in 1943 by

[1] See G. P. Valeriano, *De litteratorum infelici-
tate*, Venetiis, 1620, p. 86; L. Pastor, *History of the
Popes*, viii, London, 1908, p. 213.

[2] The MS. is in the library of the Società di
Storia Patria; the text was edited, with an introduction, by F. Volpicella, Naples, 1868.

[3] See E. Müntz, *La Bibliothèque du Vatican au
XVIe siècle*, Paris, 1886, p. 64.

[4] Paris: Bibl. Nat., MS. Fonds lat. 8401. See

L. Dorez, *Le Psautier de Paul III*, Paris, 1909,
pp. 89–90, pl. XXXIII.

[5] *Epist. Fam.* xxiii.

[6] Cf. especially *Cenno paleografico del terzo
periodo della storia della scrittura latina*, Napoli,
1899; 'Notizia della scrittura umanistica nei
manoscritti e nei documenti napoletani del XVo
secolo', in *Atti della R. Accademia di Archeologia,
Lettere e Belle Arti*, xx. ii, Napoli, 1899, pp. 1–18.

Mr. Stanley Morison. His observations were embodied in a long, valuable and amply illustrated article 'Early humanistic script and the first roman type', contributed to *The Library*, N.S. xxiv, Nos. 1–2. There will be found, in convenient and easily accessible form, some account of the initial steps by which 'this originally personal script, written by a few scholars in their respective individual styles, was developed into a general calligraphic form by a numerous body of professional scribes towards the middle of the fifteenth century'. Mr. Morison's paper owed something (though not more than was abundantly acknowledged) to Alfred Hessel's 'Die Entstehung der Renaissanceschriften', in *Archiv für Urkundenforschung*, xiii, 1935; and to the findings of B. L. Ullman, *Ancient Writing and Its Influence*, New York, 1932.

The tenth-century manuscript of Horace [1] acquired by Petrarch in 1347 and now in the Laurentian Library, Morison regards as a *pièce à clef*. As much might perhaps be said of half a dozen other books from the poet's shelves; but the name of Horace is a potent symbol. Morison goes on to suggest, with every colour of probability, and with reference to an important document in which Antonio di Mario the Florentine notary is mentioned, the commanding authority of Niccolò Niccoli, which imposed upon gifted amateurs like Poggio, and not so gifted professionals like di Mario, a discipline and a formal standard based on manuscripts like Petrarch's Horace, which were to become habitual and permanent. Just how permanent, Niccoli himself could scarcely have foreseen. With the help of Morison, a passing glance at the origins of humanistic script reveals some useful general principles for the study of its later development. It is important to bear in mind the existence of literary or antiquarian coteries and the influence on scribal practice of dominant personalities within those coteries, of men who were amateurs *quoad* the art of writing (first the learned, then the professional pen); another factor to be considered is the growth of scripts for special purposes.

Before proceeding to what W. M. Lindsay would call 'the panorama of the showman', I may be expected to justify the seemingly arbitrary limits which I have chosen to impose on the present study. The termini 1460–1560 comprise the century between the death of Poggio[1] and the publication of Gianfrancesco Cresci's *Essemplare*.[2] In thus prescinding from the early period,

---

[1] †1459.   [2] See *infra*, pp. 33 n. 3, 47–48.

where so much is still dark and doubtful, I may disappoint; I may even be blamed for having preferred the chicken to the egg. But in the first place it would be impertinent to offer, as I should be largely constrained to do, an acknowledged transcript of Mr. Morison's paper; though I welcome the present occasion to confess my obligation to it. In the second place I should consider that I used my readers with less than candour if I presumed to dilate on manuscripts of which I had not myself perused the originals. Certainly, the more facsimiles we can have the better. But the advanced student will not need to be reminded of the importance, wherever possible, of going behind the facsimiles, to the codices themselves; and more important still, to their every page, from title to colophon. The danger of basing final judgements on facsimiles, or on single pages, can hardly be over-stressed.

By the middle of the fifteenth century, the humanistic *lettera antica* or roman had acquired, in the hands of professional copyists, a momentum of its own, soon to carry its influence throughout the Italian peninsula and beyond. As early as 1434, skilful foreigners like the German Michael de Salvaticis, notary to the Venetian Senate, were learning to write the script, as is seen in the colophon (gold in the original) to a manuscript of the Dialogue of Fra Lodovico di Strassoldo of Forlì [2], made in that year for presentation to the Emperor Sigismund.[1] The script is not without faint gothic reminiscences; or, in the majuscules, rustic traces which were to disappear a generation later. In 1450 an Eusebius [3] written at Padua by an unknown scribe has pages set out in the strictest inscriptional form.[2] But it is in the sixties that humanistic script reflects, unmistakably, the changes which had begun to operate upon the spirit of humanism itself—its shifting focus; the diffusion, and sometimes the dilution, of its ideas; the logical developments of, and accretions to them. The philosophic temper of humanist Florence—literary, speculative, Platonic, always tending to abstraction—had acquired in its transit to north Italy an empiric cast, not inappropriate to the cultural ambit of that Aristotelian stronghold, Padua; nor surprising

[1] MS. Vat. Chig. D.VI.97. See A. Campana, 'Un nuovo dialogo di Lodovico di Strassoldo O.F.M. (1434)', in *Miscellanea Pio Paschini = Lateranum*, N.S. xv. 1–4, Romae, 1949, pp. 127–56.

[2] Venice: Bibl. Marc. MS. Cl.9.1. MSS. of Eusebius are, in this and other respects, peculiar, betraying the influence of a common archetype. The oldest known Latin text of Eusebius is in the Bodleian Library (MS. Auct. T.2.26, s.c. 20632). For the traditional 'layout' of the *Chronica*, see R. Helm, 'Eusebius, Chronik und ihre Tabellenform', in *Abhandlungen der preussischen Akademie der Wissenschaft*, Phil. Hist. Klasse, 1°, 1923, p. 4.

in an area so rich in the lapidary vestiges of ancient Rome. We shall have occasion, at a later stage in our inquiry, to develop this thesis. For the moment let it suffice to say, that from the antiquarian interest in classical inscriptions, first explicit in north Italy *circa* 1465, dates a significant change in Italian calligraphic practice. Thenceforward scribes began to assimilate the conventions of classical Roman capitals, first to the majuscules, and later, partly as a result of typographical influence, to the minuscules of humanistic script; transforming the blunt and rather amorphous terminal of the early caroline model, the tentative brackets of the later,[1] into the sharp clear serif which seems to 'clinch' the letters, as a good rhyme compacts a verse [4].

One result of this change in calligraphic technique was to induce a greater care and deliberation in the formation of the minuscules; to encourage the tendency to make the letters separately; and to increase their scale in relation to the page. Hence the closely concatenated pattern, which is one of the chief beauties of the *lettera antica* in its orthodox Florentine form, had begun to disintegrate, noticeably at Bologna, towards the end of the century. There, a page of writing often suggests, though it does not necessarily imitate, the appearance of a page of print. The work of Pierantonio Sallando, a native of Reggio in Emilia, who practised his art chiefly in Bologna, illustrates this later development of the *lettera antica* [5], which came to be known in the sixteenth century as *lettera antica tonda*, or round *antica*.[2]

Other influences conduced to carry the script of humanism beyond the intention of its founders; to transform an originally private literary enthusiasm into a fashionable cult. Wealth and power were accumulating in Italy, and the Renaissance had created an epoch of taste. The princely patron and the cultivated bibliophile (functions not then, as now, divisible)—the Medici at Florence; the Este at Ferrara; the Gonzaga at Mantua; the Sforza at Milan; the Aragonese kings at Naples[3]—with their insatiable demands on

---

[1] 'In general it [humanistic script] resembles Carolingian of the tenth and eleventh centuries rather than that of the ninth or twelfth.' B. L. Ullman, op. cit., p. 141.

[2] For this scribe, and a discussion of *antica tonda* script, see J. Wardrop, 'Pierantonio Sallando and Girolamo Pagliarolo', &c., in *Signature*, N.S. 2, London, 1946, pp. 4–30; also, for Sallando,

A. Mercati, *Saggi di storia e letteratura*, i, Roma, 1951, pp. 43–45.

[3] For the manuscript collections and the scribes of (*a*) the Medici, see Bandini's catalogue of the Laurentian Library; P. d'Ancona, *La miniatura fiorentina (secoli xi–xvi)*, Firenze, 1914; G. Biagi, *Reproductions from Illuminated Manuscripts, fifty plates*, Firenze, 1914; (*b*) the Este, H. J.

the services of the scribe, fostered the immense trade in fine manuscripts to which the Florentine bookseller, Vespasiano da Bisticci, was the able and genial minister.[1] The last quarter of the fifteenth century was the heyday of the richly illuminated manuscript—that perfect coalition of art and learning. It was also the classic period of the great amanuenses, few of whom perhaps had ever seen a Carolingian codex, triumphing in spite of print:[2] Antonio Sinibaldi, the rascal scribe of Medicean Florence;[3] the amorist Sigismondo de' Sigismondi, Count Palatine, of Carpi;[4] Giovanmarco Cinico, called Velox, of Parma;[5] the gossiping, Pepysian, indolent Matteo

Hermann, 'Zur Geschichte der Miniaturmalerei am Hofe der Este in Ferrara', in *Jahrbuch der Kunsthistorischen Sammlungen des Kaiserhauses*, xxi, Wien, 1900, pp. 117 et seq.; G. Bertoni, *La biblioteca Estense e la coltura ferrarese ai tempi di Duca Ercole I (1471–1505)*, Torino, 1903; idem. 'Notizie sugli amanuensi degli Estensi nel quattrocento', in *Archivium Romanicum*, ii, Genève, 1918, pp. 29–57; D. Fava, *La biblioteca Estense nel suo sviluppo storico*, Modena, 1925; (c) the Gonzaga, P. Torelli and A. Luzio, *L'archivio Gonzaga di Mantova*, Ostiglia; Verona, 1920, p. 22; (d) the Sforza, F. Malaguzzi-Valeri, *La corte di Lodovico il Moro*, Milano, 1913–23; (e) the Aragonese kings, G. Mazzatinti, *La biblioteca dei re d'Aragona in Napoli*, Rocca San Casciano, 1897; T. de Marinis, *La biblioteca napoletana dei re d'Aragona*, Milano, 1947.

[1] See his memoirs, *Vite di uomini illustri del secolo XV* (ed. P. d'Ancona and E. Aeschlimann), Milano, 1951. Of the sums expended on illuminated MSS. by Renaissance princes, it is difficult to speak precisely; and to express any amount in terms of modern currency is a task for the actuary rather than the historian. Most estimates are vague and conflicting; and all depends on the basis adopted by the assessor, which is not always known. The MS. collection of Federigo, Duke of Urbino, numbering some 2–3,000 volumes, was valued at 30,000 gold ducats. An illuminated Petrarch of superlative quality, consumed in the Burning of the Vanities at Florence on Shrove Tuesday 1497–8, was worth, in the estimation of a witness, Fra Pacifico Burlamacchi, 50 scudi. There is a useful note on monetary equivalents in the latest English edition of Burckhardt (London; Oxford (Phaidon Press), 1944, p. 53). I have read, without marking, a statement which puts the total expenditure of the Medici family, on MSS.

alone, at one million pounds sterling. See, in this connexion, E. Piccolomini, 'Delle condizioni e delle vicende della libreria Medicea privata, &c.', in *Archivio Storico italiano*, 3rd ser. xix, Firenze, 1874, pp. 101–29, 254–81.

[2] See J. Wardrop, 'Pierantonio Sallando', &c., loc. cit., pp. 6, 24–26.

[3] The only contemporary account of Sinibaldi, so far traced, is from the pen of a political opponent, Simone Filipepi, brother of Botticelli. He speaks of the scribe as 'maggiore ribaldo', who died 'in grandissima calamità et miseria'. For the chronicle of Simone Filipepi, see P. Villari and E. Casanova, *Scelta di prediche e scritti di Fra Gerolamo Savonarola*, Firenze, 1898. For Sinibaldi's script see G. Biagi, *Il carattere 'umanistico' di Ant. Sinibaldi e il libro bello*, Milano, 1922; and for a criticism, S. Morison in *The Fleuron*, ii, London, 1924, p. 72. For MSS. of Sinibaldi, cf. L. V. Delisle, *Le Cabinet des manuscrits de la Bibliothèque Impériale*, Paris, 1868–81; G. Mazzatinti, op. cit., *passim*; P. d'Ancona, op. cit.; T. de Marinis, op. cit.

[4] For the love-letters composed and transcribed by Sigismondo (Florence: MS. Laur. Plut. 43. XXV), see Bandini. Despite the claims of the writer, they did not spring, apparently, from a profound level of experience. For some account of Sigismondo, see G. Bertoni, *La biblioteca Estense*, &c., p. 264; and for his MSS., P. d'Ancona, op. cit.; G. Mercati, *Codici latini Pico Grimani Pio* (Studi e Testi, 75), Città del Vaticano, 1938, pp. 52–53. Cf. also J. Wardrop in *The Book Collector*, i. 2, London, 1952, pp. 84–90.

[5] See, besides G. Mazzatinti and T. de Marinis, op. cit., A. Altamura, 'La biblioteca Aragonese e i manoscritti inediti di Giovan Marco Cinico', in *Bibliofilia*, xli, Firenze, 1940, pp. 418–26.

Contugi of Volterra,[1] who lodged at the Lily & Angel in Ferrara, whom Leon Battista Alberti admonished 'take up thy pen and write';[2] Gianrinaldo Mennio of Sorrento, to whom in 1496 Federico of Aragon accorded, by way of pension, victuals for life and an annual suit of clothes[3]—and many more whose works can be traced, and glimpsed in facsimile, in the great collections of Hermann,[4] D'Ancona,[5] and De Marinis.[6] It was they, Sigismondo and the rest, who, however diverse their personal affinities, absorbed and retained, and carried over almost intact into the first decade of the sixteenth century, the Florentine norm for the *lettera antica*; that is to say a script which might have passed, in all material respects, the critical scrutiny of Poggio himself.

Three manuscripts serve as illustrations of this script: first, a Sallust (B.M. Add. MS. 16422) written at Florence in 1466 by Cerasius or Ciriagio [6]; secondly, a Josephus (B.M. Harley MS. 3699) written at Florence in 1478 by the pessimist who concealed his identity in the motto OMNIVM RERVM VICISSITUDO EST [7]; and thirdly, a little Horae, measuring only 4 by 3 inches, written at Carpi in 1498 by the great Sigismondo de' Sigismondi, formerly belonging to Sir Sydney Cockerell.

In dealing with manuscripts of the 'luxury' class in the period 1465–1510, it is often a matter of some nicety, in default of other helps such as a colophon or a coat of arms, to detect in them a provincial origin, or to assign to them a precise date.[7] To observe and codify, with an eye to parent scripts, regional variations in the *lettera antica*, eliminating on the way their greatest common factors, would be a worthy occupation for an advanced student of palaeography.

---

[1] Son of the jurist Ercolano (di maestro Piero di Puccino) di Contugio. Some of the personal correspondence of this scribe has survived. Letters of Contugi are printed in *Il bibliofilo*, x, Bologna, 1889, pp. 43, 44, 112, and by A. Luzio and F. Renier, 'I Filelfo e l'umanismo alla corte dei Gonzaga', in *Giornale storico della letteratura italiana*, xvi, Torino, 1890, pp. 154–7. Contugi's letters to Benedetto Dei, discovered in the Vatican Library in 1949 (MS. Vat. Lat. 9063, ff. 112–34) are, with one exception, unpublished. For a relevant note, see J. Wardrop in *The Times Literary Supplement*, 27 May 1949, p. 347. For MSS. written by Contugi, see the index to Stornajolo's catalogue of the *Fondo Urbinato*.

[2] *Bibliofilo*, x. 112.

[3] N. Barone, 'Notizia della scrittura umanistica', &c., loc. cit., p. 6.

[4] *Beschreibendes Verzeichnis der illuminierten Handschriften in Österreich*, N.S. vi: *Die Handschriften . . . der italienischen Renaissance*, Wien, 1930–3.

[5] Op. cit.

[6] Op. cit.

[7] For the latter purpose, suggestions may be found in J. P. Elder, 'Clues for the dating of Florentine humanistic manuscripts', in *Studies in Philology*, xliv. 2, 1947, p. 127.

It would not, I imagine, be unfair to say that most people, when they think of 'humanistic script' at large, do so in terms of the sumptuous codices, written in *lettera antica* and with all the attendant apparatus of border, miniature, and rubric to which we have just referred; and which, not unnaturally, are given prominence wherever Renaissance manuscripts are exhibited or reproduced. Such generalized pictures are misleading, for they distract our attention from the essential business of humanism. Those great books are the ejects of an opulent society, delicately savouring the intellectual banquet, perhaps not always mindful of the *principia*, the fundamental brainwork, in Rossetti's phrase, that made the banquet possible; and we ourselves must not be tempted to linger at the feast. Behind it, the solid work of humanism—the study of classical literature and classical remains—was pressed forward in the spirit of its founders by a numerous body of scholars, famous or obscure, throughout the whole course of the fifteenth century.

The business of humanism—the *Humanistisches in Humanismus*, as the Germans would say—was largely conducted in the cursive variant of the *lettera antica*, the variant later to win permanence through the typographical initiative of Aldus Manutius, under the familiar name of *italic*. If there are still wide gaps in our knowledge of the formal *antica*, we know still less of its informal analogue; and that despite its longer history; its possibly purer ancestry; and its survival as the latent basis of our handwriting. Informality is the keynote of italic; rapidity its virtue; utility its aim. The student might bear that tricolon in mind; remembering also that each of the qualities named is susceptible of changes in degree. Italic was in its early and middle forms a modest and unpretentious script, almost always small in scale, written with a hard narrow rounded pen, giving little differentiation between thick and thin strokes. It could be more or less rounded or compressed; sloped or upright as the writer pleased. From 1400 to 1500 its essential structure had scarcely altered.

The origins of italic are still unsettled; its variations unclassified; and many of its special uses untraced. Systematic study of the subject has not been notably advanced by the large amount of journalistic treatment it has received, and continues to receive; and already in the wake of that, there has piled up an encumbering detritus of error. We shall need as many advanced students of palaeography as we can muster, to help clear it away. Obvious

nonsense apart, what theories are we to accept, or discard? Are we to be-
lieve, with some apologists, that italic is the spurious issue of roman; that
italic is roman written quickly; roman conditioned by speed?—we might
write a roman quickly and see what happens. Or shall we cling to the firmer
and more attractive hypothesis of Schiaparelli,[1] that italic is simply the
gothic cursive under humanistic influence; that there was an italic before
there was a roman; and that there would have been an italic even had there
been no roman? Would we be content, if an angel were to present us with
a chronologically arranged series of papal briefs, to write *finis* to the story;
or should we not rather thank our heavenly visitant for closing one fascinat-
ing chapter in the history of diplomatic? Or shall we conclude that the first
humanists, when they formed their cursive script, had an eye on the glossarial variants of caroline; or even (what is not impossible) on the glossarial
variants of the insular hand? These are some of the alternatives which,
sooner or later, would have to be weighed. All we profess to do is to suggest
some possible points of departure.

It follows that the study of the humanistic cursive will be most profitably
pursued, not in the codex *de luxe*, but in the plain text. By the plain text is
meant the codex of vellum or paper which, not necessarily passing through
the intermediary of bookseller or scriptorium, is written throughout in the
scholar's own hand;[2] or, if in that of an amanuensis, is enriched with
the owner's corrections, postils or *scholia*. The intention of such a text
would be private; or for limited circulation among pupils or friends; or,
within the appropriate period, as 'copy' for the press. During the lifetime of
Niccolò Niccoli, scholar and copyist had been, perforce, one and the same
person, because there was not yet a sufficient body of professional competence to deal, at second hand, with the business of humanism in the script
of its preference. Niccoli and Poggio had themselves to write, in *lettera antica
formata*, the 'master copies' of the precious relics they had found, while
Antonio di Mario and his fellows were struggling with the subtleties of
what, to them, was an archaic script. But when they had the knack of it,
their employers were free to pursue the equally important business of
collation and recension which, following logically upon the process of

---

[1] 'Paleografia', in *Encicl. Ital.*
[2] See, in this connexion, the important article
(first of a promised series) by A. Campana,
'Scritture di umanisti (I. Antonio Costanzi)', in
Rinascimento, i. 3–4, Firenze, 1950, pp. 227–56.

recovery, became, along with teaching, the chief function of the humanist when the period of ingathering was over.

The plain texts are to be sought of course in the centres of humanist activity. For the early period, that is to say, up to the death of Poggio, the student will turn to Florence; for the period under consideration here, in that order to Venice and Rome.

After the death of Poggio in 1459, Florence ceased to have a determining influence upon the *form* of humanistic scripts. To that extent she was conservative. The city of Ficino, of Politian and Pico della Mirandola, just then embarking on her long flirtation with Plotinus, was still, indeed, prolific of ideas. But whereas ideas may engender scripts, it is with letters that they are written. If there is little evidence to show that the scribes of Medicean Florence gave time to meditation on the principles of their craft, it was otherwise at Venice.

The significance of Venice—that is to say the whole Venetian territory, the Veneto—in the history of humanism has been generally underrated, ceding far too much to the more obvious claims of Florence and Rome.[1] But it is to the Veneto, with its traditional love of experiment and innovation, that we must look for the beginnings of that concern for the historical forms, and the technical subtleties of lettering, European and Asiatic, which were so profoundly to affect the course of Italian calligraphy, especially in its cursive styles. We touched, in an earlier paragraph,[2] upon a change in Italian scribal practice, apparent *circa* 1465, whereby the capitals used for titles and headings were brought into conformity with the classical pattern, a practice later extended to the minuscules of the *lettera antica*. In summary fashion we referred this change to the growing Renaissance interest in classical inscriptions. That interest, and its extension throughout Italy, can be traced to a group of antiquaries, scholars and artists, operating chiefly in, or from, the cities of Verona and Padua: Ciriaco of Ancona;[3] Felice Feliciano of Verona;[4] Giovanni Marcanova of Padua;[5] Fra Giovanni Giocondo of Verona;[6] Bartolomeo Sanvito[7] and Andrea Mantegna,[8] both of Padua. These pioneer epigraphers—spiritual ancestors of Mommsen, Huelsen, and De Rossi—

---

[1] '. . . even before Petrarch was born, the first coherent group of Italian humanists had already formed in the Veneto . . .'. G. Billanovich, 'Petrarch and the textual tradition of Livy', loc. cit., appendix v, p. 208.

[2] *Supra*, p. 8.

[3] See *infra*, p. 14.

[4] See *infra*, p. 16.

[5] See *infra*, p. 17.

[6] See *infra*, p. 27 et seq.

[7] See *infra*, p. 23 et seq.

[8] See *infra*, p. 17.

embodied the fruits of their researches in great manuscript collections or *sillogi*, many of which, in various recensions and often copiously illustrated, have come down to us. Patiently sought out and edited by Mommsen and his assistants, they are now textually incorporated in the volumes of the *Corpus Inscriptionum Latinarum*.[1] It is well to signalize their importance now, since we shall have occasion to mention them again.

The epigraphic value of the *sillogi* is obvious; for they constitute, *inter alia*, the only evidence for inscriptions, and monuments, since dilapidated or lost or destroyed. But it is less obvious that their palaeographical significance has been realized; and I know of no publication—none certainly in English—which, in this specific connexion, so much as deigns to mention them. The characteristic *silloge* is found either in the holograph of its compiler; or in the hand of an amanuensis working under his direction; or in that of a later copyist. These manuscripts are nearly always in the cursive hand. From a perusal of them, it becomes manifest that the writing of compiler and, by transference, amanuensis or copyist, was often influenced by the letter forms, Greek as well as Roman, in which the originals were found; and that these borrowed forms became habitual, even in contexts unconnected with epigraphy, and in the practice of scribes unacquainted with Greek. From thence proceeds the assimilation to the latin minuscule alphabet of forms alien to the strictly latin tradition; and the modification of the humanistic cursive or italic, through the necessity of deliberate and accurate copying which such specialized work involved, together with the natural animal pleasure taken in setting it out. In the work of the silloge-makers there is unmistakable evidence of joy in the task; and in their occasional exuberant treatment of the humanistic cursive they show that awareness of its decorative possibilities so uncompromisingly exploited by the great writing-masters of the sixteenth century. This is nowhere more strikingly illustrated than in the writing of Ciriaco of Ancona. Its peculiarities were first noticed, and their implications grasped, by Domenico Fava. He had been impressed by the autographs of Ciriaco lent to the great exhibition held in memory of Girolamo Tiraboschi in 1932, at the Estense Library, Modena, of which Fava was then Director. He reproduced Ciriaco's script

[1] Esp. VI. For a descriptive list of the principal *sillogi*, see G. B. De Rossi, *Inscriptiones Christianae*, &c., ii, pt. 1, Romae, 1888.

in the catalogue of that exhibition,[1] and published brief observations on it.[2]

Ciriaco, or if you prefer it *anglicé*, Cyriack, Pizzicolli of Ancona (1391–1452),[3] the friend of Pope Eugenius IV, was a merchant by profession and an epigrapher by chance. In the way of business he travelled indefatigably and widely, not only in his native country, but also through much of Greece and Asia Minor, collecting inscriptions as he went. Only fragments of his vast *silloge* remain,[4] but its text has been transmitted. The extent of Ciriaco's scholarship is doubtful and his knowledge of Greek can scarcely have been systematic. But if he was no scholar, he maintained the attitude of a scholar. His diligence was exemplary; and if he did not always understand what he was copying, the accuracy of his transcriptions, once generally suspect, has been vindicated in the unchallengeable verdict of Mommsen. Ciriaco had a sense of beauty; and his expression of it, true to the Baconian formula, showed some strangeness in the proportion. Besides the bizarre forms which he imported into his handwriting [8]—fabulous as any merchandise he ever brought from the East—he had an almost feminine partiality for coloured inks, and tinted vellums: yellow, violet, lake, green, purple, and so on, which were to fix a manuscript convention, a decade after his death, in Venice and Rome. To Ciriaco's example can be traced the complicated

[1] *Mostra di codici autografici, &c.*, Modena, 1932.

[2] In *Accademie e Biblioteche d'Italia*, vi, 1932–3, later amplified in a paper 'La scrittura libraria di Ciriaco d'Ancona' contributed to the Federici Festschrift in 1945, *Scritti di paleografia e diplomatica in onore di Vincenzo Federici*, Firenze, 1945, pp. 295–305.

[3] For the career and travels of Ciriaco, see F. Scalamonti, 'Vita di Ciriaco Anconitano', in G. Colucei, *Delle antichità Picene XV*, Fermo, 1792; E. Ziebarth, 'Cyriacus von Ancona in Samothrake', in *Mitteilungen des Kaiserlich Deutschen Archäologischen Instituts, Athenische Abteilung*, xxxi, Athen, 1906, pp. 405–14; E. Jacobs, 'Cyriacus von Ancona und Mehmed II', in *Byzantinische Zeitschrift*, xxx, Leipzig; Berlin, 1929, 30, pp. 197–202; and for his view of antiquity, and its influence, E. Ziebarth, 'Cyriacus von Ancona als Begründer der Inschriftenforschung', in *Neue Jahrbücher für das klassische Altertum*, ix, Leipzig, 1902, pp. 214–26; C. Huelsen, *La Roma antica di Ciriaco d'Ancona*, Roma,

1907. For MSS. in his hand see (besides Fava, loc. cit.) Th. Mommsen, 'Über die Berliner Excerptenhandschrift des Petrus Donatus', in *Jahrbuch der Königlichen preussischen Kunstsammlungen*, iv, Berlin, 1883, pp. 73–89; R. Sabbadini, 'Ciriaco d'Ancona e la sua descrizione del Peloponneso trasmesa da Leonardo Botta', in *Miscellanea Ceriani*, Milano, 1910, pp. 183–247 (reprinted without the plates in idem., *Classici e umanisti da codici Ambrosiani*, Firenze, 1933, pp. 1–52); P. Maas, 'Ein Notizbuch des Cyriacus von Ancona aus dem Jahre 1436', in *Beiträge zur Forschung*, i, München, 1913, pp. 5–15. A MS. Strabo in the library of Eton College (Bl.4.14) has *scholia* by Ciriaco (see M. R. James's catalogue, Cambridge, 1895, no. 141); and there is a passage copied by him from Gregory of Nazianzus, in Greek and Latin, at ff. 172v–173 of a Notitia Dignitatum in the Bodleian Library (MS. Canon. misc. 378).

[4] His so-called *Commentarii* perished in the fire which destroyed the library of Alessandro and Costanzo Sforza at Pesaro in 1514.

battery of ligatures and compendia which were to become the stock-in-trade of northern scribes, and the calligraphic hall-mark, for half a century, of Padua and Verona. Certainly Ciriaco deserves to stand, by the validity of his contribution to it, near the presiding spirits of the Renaissance.

If in Ciriaco's nature there was some strangeness, it was redoubled in the person of his admirer and calligraphic legatee, Felice Feliciano of Verona. There is a temptation to linger over the odd fantastic character of Felice Feliciano (*c.* 1432–80), who is only now beginning to emerge from the obscurity to which five heedless centuries had consigned him. Antiquary; doggerel poet; calligrapher; printer; alchemist and immoralist, his literary remains lie almost entirely inedited, and he still awaits a biographer. In 1936 A. Khomentovskaia made a cumbersome and inconclusive attempt to father upon him the *Hypnerotomachia* of Poliphilus[1]; and more recently a superficial survey of some of his manuscripts has come from the scarcely lighter pen of Laura Pratilli.[2] The first hint in English of reviving interest in Feliciano was given by Victor Scholderer in the *Gutenberg Jahrbuch* for 1933. Almost all that is at present known of his life derives from the *Novelle Porretane* of Sabadino degli Arienti,[3] in whose lively pages the reader will learn (among other diverting and Rabelaisian matter) that he was known as Felix the Antiquarian; how the taint of necromancy, if not the suspicion of lunacy, hung ever about him; how he would suddenly and mysteriously disappear from his lodging to go searching for rare metals—antimony and tin—among the foot-hills of the Veronese Alps, returning after days of absence, redolent of who knows what salacious encounter by the way, penniless, dirty, dishevelled, unshaven, walking as one in a dream, with the dogs yelping at his heels and the urchins pelting him with stones. There are other testimonies to his bohemian and improvident ways: his own brother, in a letter as far as I am aware unpublished, contained in Harley MS. 5271, upbraids him as 'unstable, a vagabond here today and there tomorrow;

---

[1] 'Felice Feliciano comme l'auteur de l'Hypnerotomachia Poliphili', in *Bibliofilia*, xxxvii, Firenze, 1935, pp. 154 et seq., 200 et seq.; and xxxviii, 1936, pp. 20 et seq., 92 et seq.

[2] 'Felice Feliciano alla luce dei suoi codici', in *Atti del Reale Instituto Veneto di scienze, lettere ed arti*, xcix, 2, Venezia, 1940, pp. 33–105.

[3] Cf. also G. Fiocco, 'Felice Feliciano amico degli artisti', in *Archivio Veneto-Tridentino*, ix,

Venezia, 1926, pp. 188–99; H. Mardersteig, 'Nuovi documenti su Felice Feliciano', in *Bibliofilia*, xli, Firenze, 1940, pp. 102–10; and, for particular items in the Feliciano canon, G. Gerola, 'Codicetto Trentino del 1475 a fregi silografati', in *Accademie e Biblioteche d'Italia*, viii. 1, Roma, 1934, pp. 39–42; A. Campana, 'Felice Feliciano e la prima edizione del Valturio', in *Maso Finiguerra*, xviii, xix, fasc. 3, Milano, 1940, pp. 211–22.

fantastic, prodigal, an imitator of difficult things; an alchemist, a time-waster and a spendthrift on every vain and foolish enterprise', words worthy of Tam o' Shanter's wife, and in which a lady of my acquaintance has professed to find a portrait of her husband. It seems fairly certain that there was a screw loose in Felice Feliciano; and he was not a scholar in any sense of the term. His grammar and syntax, in Italian, are often faulty; and his Latin is deplorable. But he was, in his fashion, an artist, and the friend of artists. The man who had gained the esteem—one can hardly suppose it to have been the entire confidence—of Andrea Mantegna and Giovanni Marcanova cannot have been a fool. Readers of Kristeller's life of Mantegna will remember the *Jubilatio* of Felice Feliciano.[1] The story has been quoted by Sandys and other writers, but it will bear a further telling. Feliciano relates how, in the company of Mantegna and others, he set out blithely one Autumn day in 1464 on an antiquarian excursion along the shores of Lake Garda, visiting on the way the ruined temple of Diana, copying inscriptions here and there, and making merry with music and wine; how, later, crowned with myrtle and ivy and playing on instruments as they went, the company took ship from Desenzano to Sirmione (*O venusta Sirmio!*), as Catullus had done before, and Tennyson was to do after them. There, in the little church of San Pietro, the antiquarians gave thanks for the harvest of two and twenty inscriptions which had crowned with success their happy expedition.

A score at least of Feliciano's manuscripts have survived;[2] and it may be that as many more lie unsuspected in the libraries of Europe and America. The style of those is not easily mistaken. Some are epigraphic, most of them miscellaneous in character. To them he appropriated wholesale the mannerisms of Ciriaco [9]—the tinted pages and inks; the exotic forms and ligatures—but all his manuscripts, whether epigraphic or not in intention, bear witness to the direct observation [10], and in one instance at least the accurate measurement, of classical Roman capitals.[3] He wrote these as to the manner born; and only one scribe was to excel him in dexterity and verve. As was so justly said, in another connexion, of Marliani: 'ce n'est qu'en

---

[1] See G. Fiocco, *op. cit.*, pp. 191–192.

[2] For a partial list of these, see A. Khomentovskaia, and L. Pratilli, loc. cit. There are, besides Harley 5721 (*ut supra*), four other MSS. of Feliciano in English libraries, viz.: British Museum Add. MS. 47681 (formerly Holkham MS. 480); Bodleian Library MSS. Canon. Ital. 15 and 56; Holkham MS. 521.

[3] MS. Vat. Lat. 6852.

profitant de son travail qu'on est parvenu à le surpasser'. To all he derived, Felice Feliciano added something that was quite his own. Of his decoration we are not at present to treat (see, for example, the typical frontispiece of 1461 formerly at Holkham [12 & 13] and that of an unknown Veronese scribe showing his influence [11] formerly in the collection of Sir Sydney Cockerell). If it is sometimes coarse, and grotesque, and repellent, it is part and parcel of a man who, we may be sure, was himself often coarse, and grotesque, and repellent. But among the minor figures of the Renaissance, he shows the pervasive influence of its spirit, even on subjects to whom the true bases of culture were denied.

CHAPTER II

Humanistic Cursive as a Book-hand: Bartolomeo Sanvito

In the last chapter we declared and defined our purpose to follow, for the period 1460–1560, the broad lines in the development of humanistic writing, with particular reference to its cursive forms. These lines are most firmly impacted, and therefore most tutelary, not where they traverse the terrain of princely courts, but where they lie athwart the academic centres of humanism itself. There, in the sequestered study of the scholar; by the light of his lamp, and from the evidence of his own handwriting, are we most likely to come at the essence of humanistic scripts; to detect the seminal principle, that which is most humanistic, in them. Scholastic groups or coteries were important; and single personalities within them, inspiring by their example the emulation of disciples; affecting, as they had anticipated, professional practice within the immediate sphere of their influence, and beyond it. This process was at work in Florence, with Niccolò Niccoli as its motor; and in Venice, where Ciriaco of Ancona and Felice Feliciano, imbued with the antiquarian and artistic spirit of the region, helped, on the one hand to restore the authority of the inscriptional capital; and on the other, partly through the strong individuality, not to say the eccentricity, of their characters, to introduce an element almost of levity into the pattern of the written page.

We are now to trace the fortunes of the humanistic cursive to Rome, where it long and greatly prospered; though levity, there, is scarcely its keynote. In the nurture and admonition of Mother Church, the script suffered some of her restraints, even her astringencies. Though not the creature of the curia it became her bondman—*servus servorum Dei*. In another place something is to be said of its conveyance (through northern channels as will be suggested) to curial usage.[1] Meanwhile, adhering to our chosen formula, we are to consider the script as the servant of scholarship,

---

[1] See *infra*, p. 40 et seq.

in the characteristic style developed in the Roman Academy, under the influence of its founder, Giulio Pomponio Leto.

The name of Pomponio Leto, or Pomponius Laetus, so eminent in the history of classical scholarship, it would be superfluous, in that connexion, to emphasize here. But since the extent of his influence on the handwriting and on the book scripts of humanism is only now beginning to be appreciated in Italy,[1] it is scarcely surprising that it has passed quite unnoticed in England. I know of no English work that offers a specimen of his script; only one in which, in the character of scribe, he makes an appearance, and that of the most perfunctory kind. Yet from 1465 when he first reigned in Rome, until 1497 when he died, he did most powerfully sway his learned contemporaries. In the last quarter of the century—the twilight of humanism as it has been called—there is scarcely a figure of any note who did not frequent him, and bear away from the contact the impress of his teaching. Worthy of imitation in all things, his pupils thought him; and not least in his handwriting.

Pomponio Leto, happy in name, has been less happy in his biographer. The only modern, and therefore indispensable, source for his life was published in three well-illustrated volumes at Grottaferrata and Rome in 1909–12. It was the work of a variously gifted but eccentric Russian, Vladimir Zabughin. It bears, throughout, the evidences of titanic industry; but partakes also of what Dr. Johnson would have called the anfractuosities of the Slav mind; and to find one's way about the book—even in places to make head or tail of it—is an enterprise of some complexity, and not infrequent disappointment. The index is incomplete and, such as it is, chaotic. The notes are a nightmare. A further stumbling-block is the reported discrepancy between the original edition in Russian, often cited in footnotes but which no one appears to have seen, and the later Italian version. So presumably unless the reader has Russian, he is still far from knowing the whole truth of the matter, or what Mr. Zabughin would be at. His work is, as the French say, *tout à refaire*. A note on Pomponio's character and circumstances may therefore not be amiss.

Bastard issue in 1428 of the noble house of Sanseverino, he was the near-kinsman of the condottiere Roberto di Sanseverino, Count of Caiazzo, who

---

[1] See G. Muzzioli, *Due nuovi codici autografi di Pomponio Leto. (Contributo allo studio della scrittura umanistica)*, Roma [privately printed], 1948; A. Campana, 'Scritture di umanisti', loc. cit.

bore on his escutcheon the motto *nostro è il mestiere*—ours is the job. Certainly, Pomponio made it clear beyond a peradventure what he believed to be the business of life. In his passionate devotion to learning; his essential humility; and, in its proper place, his pride, he is the perfect type of the scholar. When, in middle age, his fame filled the peninsula, and the family which had spurned him wrote begging for his illustrious presence among them, he sent the laconic and famous reply 'quod petitis fieri non potest'. Founder of the Roman Academy *circa* 1460, Professor of Humanity at the Sapienza in 1465 and again in 1473, he is one of the world's great teachers, inspiring as he did, not only the reverence but the affection of his pupils, who spoke of, and tenderly remembered him, as 'Pater Pomponius'. Vat. Lat. 3415 is a pupil's notebook with a caricature of the master [14]. Like many of the world's great teachers, he was in person unimpressive, with a scholar's stoop and a nervous stammer. His house on the Quirinal, filled with antiquities—among them a choice cabinet of coins and medals, and the inscriptions which can be read today in the *C.I.L.*—was the meeting-place of the studious from half Europe. The story is told, how in the season of the *gran caldo*, his pupils would await him on the level ground, just before dawn; their patience was presently rewarded by the sight of his lantern, a tiny point of light traversing the hillside as, book in hand, he came down to them, bearing from another Sinai the tables of the law. The metaphor is not idle, nor essentially inappropriate; for in matter of latinity he was supreme legislator to a generation of the learned.[1] 'Pontifex Maximus' was his academic title, assumed or conferred. That was perhaps his undoing.

Pope Paul II has been represented as the friend and promoter of humane studies. He had, to be sure, some of the instincts of the scholar; some of the habits of the dilettante. But he was besides jealous, suspicious and (let us face it) cowardly and cruel. The severity of his penal reforms leaves little doubt on that score: his sudden and savage attack on the Roman humanists in 1467 gives it point. That he came to view them with hatred and distrust cannot, in the light of his acts, be questioned: that the humanists, for their

---

[1] It may be relevant here to recall that the culture of fifteenth-century Italy was predominantly Latin. Pomponio Leto was past middle life before he began the study of Greek; he is even said to have resisted its influence, for the surely unprecedented reason that it would spoil his Latin style. The great Greek scholars of the Renaissance, Politian excepted, belonged to the sixteenth century; the Greek renaissance itself, to the eighteenth—and to the Germany of Winckelmann, Lessing, and Goethe.

part, had courted his animosity is equally certain. Their paganism—no more culpable, perhaps, than Swinburne's—had been too loudly proclaimed. The secret meetings in the catacombs, innocent in effect, were conspiratorial in appearance. The academic *noms de guerre*—Mincinius, Pantagathus, Papirius —smacked of freemasonry.[1] To Paul, in his disposition to see the worst, the humanists must have seemed, at best, insolent, arrogant, too clever by half. Pontifex Maximus indeed! It was time to teach them a sharp lesson. The Pope began by dissolving the Roman Academy, and arresting its chief members on a charge of conspiring against his life. That the accusation had any basis in reality, not the most partial of apologists would nowadays venture to affirm. The pattern is only too familiar: the fabricated testimony; the swift nocturnal arrest; the extorted confession. While the case went forward in Rome, the putative ringleader, Leto himself, awaited, in a Venetian prison, his trial on another charge. The evidence for that seems to have rested on some letters, injudiciously written to a youthful pupil, of the kind that Winckelmann and others after him have written, to youthful pupils. At the Pope's instance Leto was extradited, and together with his friends Bartolomeo Platina, Demetrio Guazzelli of Lucca,[2] Partenio Minuzio Paolino[3] and others thrown into Castel Sant'Angelo. There it remained for the amiable pontiff to have them put to the torture. Platina, in his *Lives of the Popes*, tells how the vaults of Hadrian's tomb resounded to their groans, which he compares to those of the victims whom Phalaris roasted in the brazen bull. All—Leto, Platina, Guazzelli and the rest— survived the rough manicure.[4] Strangely enough, it did not noticeably affect their handwriting. They all wrote beautifully, and they all wrote alike.

In an impoverished youth, and at a time when the distinction between amateur and professional was narrow, Pomponio Leto had not scorned the *métier* of copyist.[5] He signed none of his *juvenilia* and many of them are not

[1] For another view, see G. Lumbroso, 'Gli academici nelle catacombe', in *Archivio della R. Società Romana di Storia Patria*, xii, Roma, 1889, pp. 215–39.

[2] See P. Guidi, 'Pietro Demetrio Guazzelli da Lucca, il primo custode della Biblioteca Vaticana (1481–1511)', in *Miscellanea F. Ehrle*, v, Roma, 1924, pp. 192–218.

[3] See P. de Nolhac, 'Recherche sur un compagnon de Pomponius Laetus', in *École française de Rome: Mélanges*, &c., vi, Rome, 1886, pp. 139–46.

[4] All, except Leto, broke down under the questioning: from him no confession could be extracted.

[5] See P. de Nolhac, *La Bibliothèque de Fulvio Orsini*, Paris, 1887, p. 199.

now, perhaps, identifiable, but from the enforced exercise grew a practised and subtle hand, apt to the high pursuits of the scholar. The texts which, in his function as editor, he transcribed for himself; the marginalia with which, in his character as teacher or *capo scuola*, he adorned the plain texts of his pupils, are models of grace, refinement, and fitness to purpose. He eschewed the calligraphic whimsies of a Ciriaco or a Feliciano, permitting himself but two archaisms—the medial use of uncial G and T.[1] His writing is as neat and compact as a carolingian gloss: *castigata et clara*. For him always, indefectibly, the golden mean. No scribe ever had closer imitators; and in places where both are promiscuously mixed, it is hard to disengage the script of the master from that of his pupils. The point must remain perplexed and difficult until the cataloguing of the great Fondo Fulvio Orsini in the Vatican Library, now in the able hands of Dr. Augusto Campana, is finished. A duly authenticated example of Pomponio's script is to be seen in a Silius Italicus in the Vatican [15].[2]

It is proposed to devote the remainder of this chapter to the work of a single scribe, who certainly belonged to the circle of Pomponio Leto and Platina, and absorbed much of their influence while remaining in the fullest sense original. His name, already cited incidentally, meant little or nothing until 1947; but when the extent of his work has been gauged, and its implications made explicit, he is surely destined to a high place in Renaissance studies; and chiefly in the esteem of people whom scripts, and illumination, most concern. I refer to Bartolomeo Sanvito, or de Sancto Vito, of Padua. In here presenting a thesis imperfect in detail, I have felt justified for three reasons: first, because some interest must *ipso facto* attach to the solution of a problem which engaged at least the passing attention of Theodor Mommsen;[3] secondly because some account of the consecutive steps taken in reaching that solution may be a relevant object-lesson to advanced students of palaeography; thirdly because the story of Bartolomeo Sanvito already enjoys a sort of unauthorized or subterraneous currency, and it is well that the canonical version should be known, and the responsibility for it publicly borne on the appropriate shoulders.

---

[1] For this and other orthographic peculiarities of Leto, see G. Muzzioli, op. cit. Dr. Muzzioli makes the interesting, and convincing suggestion that the use of uncial G derives from Leto's acquaintance with the famous Medicean codex of Virgil (Bib. Laur. Plut. 39. 1).

[2] MS. Vaticano Latino 3302.

[3] See *infra*, pp. 28–29.

One day, in the spring of 1947, in Rome, Dr. Augusto Campana and the author were looking through his collection of photographic facsimiles. He drew my attention to a batch, taken from manuscripts of the first class, all in the cursive hand, all apparently by the same scribe, and all unsigned. I recognized the script as one I had seen, and admired, often before, whose beauty and highly individual character, not without some of the marks of the amateur, had piqued my curiosity. I was able to assure my Italian colleague that I could match his collection with almost as many more examples drawn from sources in England and elsewhere. Three examples will serve as illustrations, one originally noted by Dr. Campana, two by myself: the great Greek and Latin Homer, MS. Vaticano Greco 1626, bearing the arms of Cardinal Francesco Gonzaga, the Greek text finished by Giovanni Rossos in 1477 [16]; the Suetonius, written for Lodovico Agneli, from the library of the Duke of Wellington [17]; and the Eusebius, Royal 14.C.3 in the British Museum, written for Bernardo Bembo, this last a fundamental document for our present argument [18]. It was clear that our independent observation was converging on a numerous and important group of manuscripts (just how numerous we did not then know) all executed, as the arms proclaimed, for patrons of the most exalted rank, and associated invariably with illuminators of the highest skill. That the unknown scribe must have been a personage of note in his time went without saying; to acquiesce in his anonymity was unbecoming. The problem faced us with a challenge. It was not until my return to England that the first ray of light was uncovered, and that by chance, in the course of a systematic examination of the manuscripts in the Library of Eton College. The first page of the little Cicero, No. 149 in M. R. James's catalogue [19a], I had known through the facsimile, showing majuscules only, in the Burlington Fine Arts Catalogue of 1908; but it was only when I had the book in my hands that I recognized in it the script, or one similar to it in all essentials, of the mysterious copyist of Rome. It differed from that in one particular: whereas Dr. Campana's selection, and most of the MSS. known to me, had shown a hand firm and perfectly controlled; this had, to quote from my own notes made on the occasion 'a distinct quaver, as if the scribe were old or ill'. To that point we shall return later.[1] Most important of all, the last page of the Eton Cicero [19b] bore initials, a place, and a date: B. S., Rome, 1497. Here

---

[1] See *infra*, p. 31.

at least was a beginning. The obvious sources of reference, from Bradley onwards, were searched in an attempt, unavailing as it proved, to find a name which, within the relevant period, would fit the initials. There the matter seemed likely to rest indefinitely, till chance again took a hand in it. Among the group of manuscripts just mentioned we referred to the documentary importance, for the purposes of our present argument, of the Eusebius, Royal 14.C.3 in the British Museum. It has proved vitally important because, unlike any of the other codices still known to us only as the work of B. S., it is written in two distinct scripts: it is obvious that in having B. S.'s italic *and* roman side by side in the same book [20], we were possessed not only of a convenient norm for both, but of a clue which doubled our chances of success. It is possible, we reasoned, that if we fail to trace an expansion of the tantalizing initials in the cursive script, we may find it in the formal *antica*. Just there, as it happened, we reasoned soundly.

It was, I suppose, another hazard which led me, some months later, to an article in the twelfth volume of *Rivista d'arte*, for the year 1930. The article, signed by Silvio De Kunert (1857–1933), dealt with the attribution to Girolamo Campagnola, of the miniatures in two manuscripts belonging to the Collegiate Church of Santa Giustina at Monselice, near Padua.[1] From the facsimiles given by De Kunert, and with Royal 14.C.3 in mind, I had no difficulty in recognizing the roman script of B. S.; and little doubt, when I had read a few lines of the text, that the key to the mystery had dropped into my hands. The manuscripts in question, an Epistolary and an Evangelary, had been written and presented to Monselice in 1509, as the colophons testified [21], by a certain Bartolomeo Sanvito, Paduan, canon of that church. De Kunert did not reproduce the colophons, but it may be instructive to consider these manuscripts. Though the qualities of the script had not escaped the notice of De Kunert, his concern was with the miniatures: he drew no palaeographical inference, nor, if he was ever aware of them, did he live to follow up the wide implications of his discovery. But it is to him that we owe almost all that is known of Sanvito; and that is considerably more than we know of almost any Renaissance scribe.

To the story of Sanvito, the *Rivista d'arte* article of 1930, though vital in its opportunity, was only incidental—the afterthought to a piece of research

[1] 'Due codici miniati da Girolamo Campagnola?', in *Rivista d'arte*, xii, Firenze, 1930, pp. 51–80.

carried out by De Kunert in 1907, and by him referred to in a footnote. In that year he published in the Bulletin of the Civic Museum of Padua, the greater part of a manuscript diary covering the years 1505–11, which he had discovered in the Archive of the Pio Istituto degli Esposti. This he entitled (I translate): 'An unknown Paduan and his diary of the early years of the sixteenth century . . . with notes on two illuminated manuscripts.'[1] The unknown Paduan was, *ut constat*, Bartolomeo Sanvito; the illuminated manuscripts, the Epistolary and Evangelary of Monselice, mentioned in the diary, and thus enabling De Kunert to trace them. His interest being almost exclusively in the miniatures of these, De Kunert did not enlarge upon the script; though his appreciation of its quality, and of the salient points in Sanvito's handwriting in so far as it was known to him, show that the defect was not due to lack of competence. It does not seem to have occurred to him, despite the evidence of the diary, that one who wrote so well might have been responsible for other works of the kind. But it would not befit us, working from *ex post facto* evidence, to cavil: De Kunert was a good scholar, and his apparatus to the diary is admirable. He set himself, in the most thorough and painstaking fashion, to unearth from the civic archives of Padua and elsewhere, all that could be found concerning his forgotten co-citizen. The details, many of them relating to property, do not interest us here. What signifies most is that Bartolomeo Sanvito was born at Padua in 1435 (of a family which, though not noble, would have appeared today in an Italian equivalent of Burke's Landed Gentry), and that he was still alive in 1518.

In one respect only did De Kunert fail to fulfil his obligations as a scholar. He did not publish Sanvito's diary in full: 'deeming it expedient' (to quote his own introductory words) 'to omit those notes which relate exclusively to simple and ordinary private or family affairs . . . *senza interesse per lo studioso*.' Fatal assumption! Nothing, as he ought to have known, is insignificant to the historian; and the omission is perhaps now irreparable. Silvio De Kunert died by his own hand at Venice on 17 June 1933.[2] Since then no trace of the manuscript diary of Bartolomeo Sanvito can be found.

Of the diary itself, as published by De Kunert, pressure of time precludes

---

[1] 'Un padovano ignoto ed un suo memoriale de' primi anni del cinquecento (1505–1511)', in *Bollettino del Museo Civico di Padova*, x, Padova, 1907, pp. 1 et seq., 64 et seq.

[2] For an obituary notice see *Ateneo Veneto*, cxxiv. v. 112 n. 3, Venezia, 1933, p. 239.

the full examination here. It is the record, consecutively kept but not on every day, of six years in the life of a retired but intellectually active man, already past seventy when he began the little book. The habit of diary-keeping is rarely acquired in old age, it is usually caught in youth, and if not abandoned there, is apt to be continued throughout life. Was De Kunert's *Memoriale* the last of a series? It is not impossible that some other fragment may survive. Meanwhile, the only evidence we possess for Sanvito's youth is an agreement dated 17 October 1466, seen and quoted by De Kunert, concerning a fresco in the Corpus Christi Chapel of San Antonio in Padua, to which the witnesses were Francesco Squarcione and Bartolomeo Sanvito, the latter of whom drew up the deed, he being then thirty-one years of age. It is a pity that this important document, which De Kunert testifies was in the hand of Sanvito, has shared the fate of the diary. It would have given us a standard by which to fix the attribution of some early manuscripts, still in doubt. At least the missing deed attests Sanvito's acknowledged competence in writing; and his simultaneous association with an artist of fame, Squarcione, the benevolent master of Mantegna.

The diary with De Kunert's notes, fundamental for the study of Sanvito, tells us something of the manner of man he was. It reveals no humble copyist, but a cultivated amateur (in both senses of the term); a man of property who has filled his cabinet with fine things—jewels; cameos; gold and silversmith's work; coins and medals; stuffs and pottery. He speaks of these with the air of one to whom their special qualities had been long familiar, and whose liberal sense of their value is expressed in willingness to lend them to his friends. There are many references to manuscripts (leaves of coloured vellum being here and there specified) some of which can be identified; and as many testimonies to a close association with artificers, painters, minia-turists, and scholars. In this connexion the name which most prominently and frequently occurs is that of the Veronese architect and epigrapher, Fra Giovanni Giocondo (1443–1515), and nearly always in relation to a *libro degli epigrammi*—epigrammi being, in the context, inscriptions. The *silloge* of Fra Giocondo, one of the most important of all epigraphic sources, exists in three distinct recensions, and in numerous manuscript copies.[1] The first recension [22], dedicated to Lorenzo the Magnificent, was begun in

[1] The most complete list of these is in A. Silvagni, *Inscriptiones christianae*, &c., i, Romae, 1922, p. xxxv et seq.

27

1478;[1] the third, subject to constant accretions and emendations on the part of its compiler and his friends, belongs to the last decade of the fifteenth, and the first of the sixteenth, centuries. The most notable representatives of the third recension (not to speak of one in Toledo which I have not seen)[2] are in England, in the collections of the Duke of Devonshire [23] and the British Museum respectively. Both were apparently unknown to Mommsen; but the Chatsworth codex was later noted by Lanciani[3] and Ziebarth.[4] Since Mommsen's time, the transcription of almost the whole constellation of manuscripts has been loosely assigned to the hand of Fra Giocondo himself, largely on the authority of De Rossi; though a glance at the script of Fra Giocondo, as authenticated from his holograph in the Vatican Library, puts the notion out of countenance. It seems to have been tacitly accepted by Mommsen, at least in so far as the first recension and the purposes of the *C.I.L.* were concerned; but it must be remembered that he was not primarily concerned with questions of autography, but of authorship. That he had his private doubts and reservations will presently appear. Of the dozen or so manuscript copies of the *silloge* of Fra Giocondo, in its three recensions, examined by Dr. Campana and/or myself, every one is wholly or in part the work of Bartolomeo Sanvito of Padua. How near Mommsen came, with his infallible instinct, to establishing the fact, is proved by a holograph letter, addressed in the pure and beautiful Italian of which he was master, to C. A. Cigogna in 1862, a twelvemonth before the first volume of the *C.I.L.* appeared. The letter, dated from Venice, 31 May, is loosely attached to the inside cover of MS. Cigogna 2704 in the Library of the Civico Museo Correr, Venice, where I copied it in 1948. That manuscript is one of the copies of Giocondo's *silloge* which is *not* in the autograph of Sanvito, though I have reason to suspect that the drawings are from his hand [24].

On the evidence of his letter, Mommsen had detected from the start the operation in the third recension of another hand: not that of a simple

---

[1] A copy on vellum, written throughout in majuscules, is in the Vatican Library (MS. Vat. Lat. 10228). See pl. 22; and for a description, with facsimile in colours, I. Carini, 'Sul codice epigrafico di Fra Giocondo recentemente acquistato dalla Biblioteca Vaticana', in *Pontificia Accademia Romana di Archeologia: Dissertazioni*, ser. ii, v, Roma, 1894, pp. 219–82.

[2] Now in the Biblioteca Nacional, Madrid (MS. 103–4). A recent comparison of this MS. with photographs from the Chatsworth *silloge* has shown the scripts to be identical.

[3] *Storia degli scavi di Roma*, i, Roma, 1902, pp. 96–98.

[4] *Ephem. Epigr.*, ix, fasc. ii, Roma, 1905, pp. 222, 241.

copyist, but of a scholar—*un altro letterato sconosciuto*, as he says; and more-over one who in his treatment of the Paduan inscriptions showed himself familiar with the contemporary state of that city, i.e. whose knowledge of the Paduan inscriptions, and references to their situation, were based apparently on long residence and direct observation. And if any doubt should remain, it is dispelled by the evidence of Stowe MS. 1016 [25].

Fra Giocondo, for his part, had in fact acknowledged the collaboration of friends in the great labour on which he was engaged. In the dedication of the first recension, to Lorenzo de' Medici, he gives a prominent place to Alessandro Cortese;[1] and in the prefatory epistle of the second, addressed to Lodovico Agneli, Archbishop of Cosenza until he was poisoned by the Borgia, he says: '. . . opus hoc . . . clementiae tuae referri debet acceptum qui ad id me etiam litteris compulisti, curante Bartholomaeo Sanvito tui amantissimo'. Further than that, Fra Giocondo does not go: he might well have added a reference to the admirable penmanship which was so constantly at his command.

We find, then, Bartolomeo Sanvito in close and lifelong relationship with one of the most famous architects and antiquaries of his age. Not less significant is his association with that great and neglected scholar and senator and proconsul, Bernardo Bembo, the father of Pietro.[2] At least four of the texts transcribed by Sanvito were made for the elder Bembo, and bear his annotations: these are the great Eusebius Royal 14.C.3 [18] and the Eton Cicero already referred to [19*a* & *b*]; an Horace at King's College, Cambridge; and a Sallust, formerly in the Chester Beatty collection; whence it passed to the Richardson collection in Boston, Massachussets; and is now, we hope, at journey's end in the Library of Harvard University. Of Sanvito's friendship with Bernardo Bembo, and its intimate character, we can offer a striking documentary proof. It is taken from folio 43 of Additional MS. 41068, the commonplace book of Bernardo Bembo—the once-celebrated

---

[1] †1491. Apostolic scriptor under Sixtus IV. See A. Sabbadini, *Storia del ciceronianismo*, Torino, 1886; F. Pintor [ed.], *Da lettere inedite di due fratelli umanisti* (*Alessandro e Paolo Cortesi*), (Nozze Savj-Lopez—Proto di Albaneta), Perugia, 1907; F. Banfi, 'Alessandro Tomasso Cortese glorificatore di Mattia Corvino', &c., in *Archivio Storico per la Dalmazia*, anno XI, xxiii, Roma, 1937, pp. 135–60.

[2] For Bernardo Bembo the chief contemporary source is the Diary of Marin Sanudo. No exhaustive modern study exists; but the following are important: V. Cian, 'Per Bernardo Bembo', in *Giornale storico della letteratura italiana*, xxviii, Torino, 1896, pp. 348–64; xxxi, 1898, pp. 49–81; A. della Torre, 'La prima ambasceria di Bernardo Bembo', ibid., xxxv, 1900, pp. 258–333.

zibaldone [26], whose loss to Italy was so long deplored by one generation of Italian scholars; whose existence is hardly known to another, since the book passed silently into the British Museum in 1924, from the heirs of George Neilson, sometime Procurator-Fiscal of Glasgow.[1] Under the inscription 'Victoria Venetianorum semper constet foeliciter' the entry in translation reads: 'from the book of inscriptions of the Reverend Dominus Bartolomeo Sanvito, my honoured compatriot, on the occasion of the birth of my son, Bartolomeo, who was born at Padua, his mother being Magnaleda, the year of our Lord'. Of Magnaleda, the *leggiadra giovinetta padovana* of Vittorio Cian,[2] nothing is known, save that she was the friend of Bernardo's youth; and since the commonplace-book covers a lifetime, there is no clue to the missing date—we can but say hail and farewell to the fair Paduan, and her natural child Bartolomeo. The note is important, first, because it shows how Sanvito stood in the estimation of a great and patrician contemporary —the Podestà of Verona and Vice-Doge of Venice was pleased to name his son after our scribe—secondly, because it demonstrates, in the most convincing manner possible, the renown which his epigraphic transcriptions enjoyed in their time.

We have not yet been able to establish for Sanvito, from documentary sources, a personal contact with Pomponio Leto; but all the available evidence, stylistic and otherwise, points to a long and close association on the part of the Paduan, with the Roman Academy and its chief members, Platina, Guazzelli, and Demetrio da Lucca. The earliest dated manuscript from Sanvito's hand, a copy of Calderini's commentary on Juvenal [27],[3] bearing the insignia of Giuliano de' Medici, was written at Rome in 1474, the year after Pomponio Leto's reappointment to the Chair of Humanity at the Sapienza; the Ciceros at Eton [19] and in the British Museum, Harley 6051 [28] and 2692, are dated from Rome, 1497, 1494 and 1498 respectively.

In an earlier paragraph we remarked that Sanvito's script is invariably found side by side with illuminations and miniatures of the highest quality. This phenomenon has led Dr. Michelini-Tocci, who was in part responsible for arranging the great quincentenary exhibition at the Vatican Library in

---

[1] See G. Neilson, 'A Venetian's commonplace book', in *Athenaeum*, London, 21 Dec. 1895, pp. 871–2; E. Levi, 'Lo zibaldone di Bernardo Bembo', in *Rassegna bibliografica della letteratura italiana*, anno IV, 2, Pisa, pp. 45–60.

[2] Loc. cit.

[3] Florence: Bibl. Laur. Plut. 53.2. It has marginalia in the hand of Politian (see Bandini).

1950, to conclude that (to quote from the English edition of the catalogue)[1] 'there was a special kind of miniature work peculiar to the Humanists who worked in the Vatican library and the Roman Academy'. It is only just to recall that this view has been long privately held by Sir Sydney Cockerell, though it has had little support from others professedly knowing in such matters. These have doubtless had in mind the dictum, emanating from a respectable source, to the effect that no style originated in Rome. But if nothing of the kind originated in Rome, all roads, as is said, lead thither. The southward way from Venice was especially crowded. One might search the members' list of Pomponio's Academy and hardly find a Roman name; but it was Rome that took them to her heart; there that they sharpened their intellects and their skills. If we are the better able now to speak of a characteristically Roman school of illumination and writing than we were five years ago, let us nevertheless suspend judgement; let us await the considered verdict of Dr. Michelini. Like all matters of wide import, it will take time.

Similarly, that part of the task which has fallen to my learned collaborator, Campana, and myself is likely to be long and operose. To speak in round numbers, some forty manuscripts, widely scattered over Europe and America, can with confidence be ascribed to the hand of Bartolomeo Sanvito. That number, which grew with spectacular rapidity, will presumably increase; for we have to do with a prolific and rapid writer who enjoyed a long life. We have to reckon with the changes which, in a long life, will affect the script of any writer, a factor which has already divided the work of Sanvito into two distinct groups. The *tremolo* noticed in the Eton Cicero, and characteristic of Sanvito's later work, much exercised us at the start: we had begun to think that we were engaged with two different scribes, until a direct reference in the diary to attacks of arthritis made all clear and dispelled our doubts. We have still to ponder carefully the claims of dubious candidates for the canon; to detach from it the work of associates and imitators, or precursors, this last a labour of peculiar nicety through the disappearance of the Malmignati archive, a private source known to De Kunert. One imitator at least we have identified: the German, Jacopo Aurelio Questenberg [29], *cubicularius* apostolic and solicitor of briefs.[2]

[1] *Miniatures of the Renaissance*, Vatican City, 1950, p. 17.

[2] See G. Mercati, 'Questenbergiana', in *Opere minori* iv, (Studi e testi 79), Città del Vaticano 1937, pp. 437–61.

Further, we have to precise, if we can, Sanvito's relations with Pomponio Leto; what his script owes to Leto, and, perhaps, what Leto's owes to Sanvito; for he was the elder man, and some reciprocity is to be supposed. The details of Sanvito's association with Fra Giocondo, the full extent, and the sequence of his contributions to the *silloge* can only be determined by collating all the known copies of that—a work in itself. And what, we are bound to ask ourselves, was the *Wandlung* of Bartolomeo Sanvito? When, if ever, did he visit the courts of the great families—the Medici, the Gonzaga, and others—who patronized his art?

We have evidence for the intervention of Sanvito's hand—as the proveditor of headings and running titles—in manuscripts which are manifestly the work of other scribes. The exquisite little Virgil, Additional MS. 11355, is a case in point [30]. Conversely, we know of one instance where a manuscript, lacking its miniatures and initials, presumably in consequence of Sanvito's death, was handed over for completion to no less an artist than Giulio Clovio: I refer to the famous Stuart de Rothesay Horae, Additional MS. 20927 [31] in the British Museum.[1] Lastly, we have traced two manuscripts which formed part of Sanvito's own library and bear his additions or marginalia: the Petrarch, Harley 3567, signed by Matteo Contugi [32]; and the Horace, Harley 3510 [33].

The Stuart de Rothesay Horae, in the formal *antica*, prompts a passing reference to the relatively small group of Sanvito's manuscripts written in that hand, and to which Royal 14.C.3[2] was the index. Typical is the Virgil, Kings 24 [34]; and the so-called Holford Petrarch, now in the possession of Mr. H. Harvey Frost [35].[3]

Our allotted space allows, though it does not license us to omit, a brief note only on the characteristics of Sanvito's manuscripts, and on the recognition symbols as it were of his cursive style. The manuscripts (turning aside from the *sillogi* which must be classed apart) are of two kinds: the opulent and magnificent folios such as the Vatican Homer [16]; the British Museum Eusebius [18]; and the Duke of Wellington's Suetonius [17], with their almost overpowering frontispieces, usually an architectural *motif*, set against a background of shredded colour, with the familiar appendages of *amorini*

[1] See British Museum: *Reproductions from Illuminated Manuscripts*, &c., ser. iv, London, 1928, p. 17, pl. L.

[2] See *supra*, p. 29.

[3] See B. Quaritch, Ltd., *A Catalogue of Illuminated and Other Manuscripts*, &c., London, 1931, pp. 98–99.

and swags and *spolia opima*, which is as near as the humanists came to a title-page. Secondly (and sharing the main characteristics of those) the 'small octavos', usually of the works of Horace or Virgil, of which typical examples are at King's College, Cambridge,[1] and Princeton University respectively.[2] In these, initial or intermediate pages of stained vellum—purple, yellow, green, and sometimes salmon-pink—are often found, a convention inherited from Ciriaco of Ancona and Felice Feliciano. To the example of that gifted Tom o' Bedlam, Sanvito would seem to owe something of his matchless skill in the free handling of Roman capitals [36]. Like Feliciano he had learned in the school of the inscriptions themselves; and to that he added an experience in copying, unparalleled in the whole compass of Italian writing. No one could set out a page of capitals as he did; and he wrote them in characteristic fashion: alternate lines of gold, blue, lake, purple, violet, and green. He who can write Roman capitals can write anything, said Gianfrancesco Cresci almost a century later.[3] Bartolomeo Sanvito ascertains the truth of the statement.

The peculiar quality of Sanvito's 'italic' hand, easily detected by the practised eye, it would be difficult to define in general terms; and we have no space here in which to conduct a minute palaeographical examination. Apart from the obvious marks of patavinity, revealed in the exaggerated *ct* and *sp* ligatures; the *h* with vowel compendia (sparingly used), and the medial use of inscriptional *Q* and uncial *T* and *G* (the latter a trick perhaps caught from Pomponio Leto),[4] there is no obvious straining after calligraphic effect. The sober and serious and practical intention of the script is everywhere apparent; and though it is manifestly the work of a born penman, it never ceases, from first to last, to be handwriting: handwriting at its highest level, but still handwriting, the handwriting (and let there be no misunderstanding) of a scholar and a gentleman, but one who has not lost the common touch. There is little difference between a Sanvito writing for Bernardo Bembo, and a Sanvito making an inventory of his property [37]. I submit that it was for that reason—because it retained the character, the idiosyncracy of the man himself, a man we may feel sure, to whom, like

---

[1] See M. R. James, *Catalogue of the Manuscripts in the Library of King's College, Cambridge*, Cambridge, 1895, no. 34, pp. 53–54.

[2] VRG MS. 2945/1400. See Walters Art Gallery, Baltimore: *Illuminated Books of the Middle Ages and the Renaissance*: Exhibition, Baltimore, 1949.

[3] *Essemplare di più sorti lettere*, &c., Roma, 1560.

[4] See G. Muzzioli, op. cit.

Horace, good manners were habitual and excess repugnant—that it won the approbation, throughout Italy, of the cultivated and the learned, and stirred their desire to possess, in permanent form, the best handwriting in the land.

The little Juvenal from the Brotherton Collection at Leeds University shows the typical plain text in which Sanvito excelled.[1] I reproduce it for the further reason that it bears, just visible on the right margin of the plate [38]—the *sigla* almost invariably present in the manuscripts of our scribe. They are contractions, reading upwards, for the Greek words ὡραῖον and σημειωτέον meaning, respectively, 'seasonable' or 'beautiful', and 'worthy of note'. T. W. Allen traces their use, in Greek manuscripts, to the ninth century, that is, to the earliest period of Greek minuscules.[2] They are endemic in the school-texts of Pomponio Leto, even in vernacular works, and wherever found are to be taken as suggesting some connexion with the master.[3]

We have already referred to Sanvito as an amateur in both senses of the term. So, it would seem, he chose to regard himself. Michelangelo extruded with a gesture of impatience the suitor who addressed him as *lo gran scultore*, preferring to be thought a gentleman first, and an artist afterwards. Congreve, a century and a half later, was of the same mind, and drew a characteristic rebuke from Voltaire. Of any such affectation Sanvito was surely free, since he half-lowered the mask of anonymity only twice; and discarded it but once, in fulfilment of a pious vow. There are two high roads to eclipse in the record of fame: one is, if you are a scholar, to publish nothing; the other, if you are an artist, not to sign your work. Sanvito seems to have taken both roads. His example is not singular. I might, with the utmost respect and relevance, cite the case of one of our most celebrated scribes of the twentieth century, Graily Hewitt, who, emeritus, octogenarian, used to remember in his Hampshire home the calligraphic glories of fifty years.[4] From a large acquaintance with his work, I can recall only two instances in which any mark of identification, or a date, appears. His fame is great, and must long continue; but it is conceivable that his lifework,

---

[1] For this MS. see R. H. Martin, in *Proceedings of the Leeds Philosophical and Literary Society, Literary and Historical Section*, vi, pt. 5, Leeds, 1948, pp. 361–3.

[2] In *Plato, Codex Oxoniensis Clarkianus 39*, &c., Lugduni Batavorum, 1898, p. vi.

[3] For a curious misinterpretation of them, see P. O. Kristeller, 'Un codice padovano di Aristotele', &c., in *Bibliofilia*, l, Firenze, 1948, p. 171.

[4] †22 Dec. 1952.

patent to any contemporary, may present a pretty problem to the curious two centuries hence. We need not marvel, then, at the name and fame of Bartolomeo Sanvito thus silted over in the process of time; but rather at what Stevenson called 'the romance of destiny' by which those have been recovered, nearly five hundred years after, 'on these ultimate islands'.

One word in conclusion before we part with Bartolomeo Sanvito. The question has been often asked, who supplied, or inspired, the design for the italic types which Francesco Raibolini cut for Aldus Manutius [39] in 1501? Typographical authorities seem to be agreed in thinking that these were not based on the script of a professional calligrapher. The amateurish quality of their design has been remarked. If a calligraphic design had been sought by Aldus, he had not far to look, since in 1501 no less a personage than Giovanantonio Tagliente had been, for almost a decade, master of writing to the Venetian Chancery.[1] Aldus did not, apparently, go to Tagliente. We do not know to whom he went. But, bearing in mind his special purpose—to provide in handy printed form, that which had hitherto been available only in handy manuscript form: the plain text of Virgil and Horace and the other classics—it is not unreasonable to suppose that he turned rather to a scholar; one of his own circle; one, moreover, whose script, in just that connexion, was famous throughout the whole Veneto, whose known texts of Virgil and Horace anticipate, in style, in 'layout', and in dimensions almost to a millimetre, those of their Aldine successors. Did Bartolomeo Sanvito, the friend of the Aldine academicians Fra Giocondo and Bernardo Bembo, the familiar of Campagnola, the type-founder associate of Aldus, did Sanvito come into the picture? If so, to what extent? His script and Aldus's type are not identical; but I know of no other script which, in form and spirit, so closely resembles it. We have a long way to go before we dare formulate a hypothesis in this sense. Nevertheless, I must leave my readers with that speculation.

[1] For Tagliente see *infra*, pp. 45-46.

CHAPTER III

From Study to Curia: Development of Chancery Cursive

'Scripts, like populations, recruit chiefly from below.' Dr. E. A. Lowe, who unites with a profound scholarship the rare gifts of wit and imagination, used something of both when he penned that pointed sentence.[1] In all pointed sentences, as another great Doctor averred, allowances have to be made. Dr. Lowe wished as it were to startle us into awareness of a principle; to remind us that scripts are not static but volatile things; that they react upon one another; that their borders are always shifting; that they intermarry for better or for worse. Scripts reflect, inevitably, the social, intellectual, and economic condition of the men who write them; and in the last quarter of the fifteenth century—the eve of convulsive changes in the state of Europe —the humanistic cursive moved with the times. From a script for special purposes it turned into a script for general purposes. The metamorphosis impelled it in two directions. First, the script made headway as a book-hand; then, it became the chosen medium of polite correspondence.

Let us examine its mutations in that order. We have already seen how Bartolomeo Sanvito of Padua, an amateur with the inborn gift of style, won, by virtue of it, a place beside the greatest illuminators of the age; and with them stepped, like a well-mannered guest, into the libraries of Princes and Counsellors. That was in the early seventies. His manuscripts of the Latin classics, so widely approved and prized, were nearly all in the cursive hand. Their acceptance at such high levels could only mean that the authority of the formal *antica* had weakened; that its powers were being delegated; that a cadet branch of the family was in the ascendant. We shall suggest, in a moment, one reason for this reversal of fortune. The promotion of the cursive could scarcely have taken place so quickly and so decisively if the cursive had been thought in any way inferior; and if our reasoning up to this point has been sound, it is not as a usurper or a *parvenu* relation

[1] In *The Legacy of the Middle Ages* (ed. C. G. Crump and E. F. Jacob), Oxford, 1926, p. 206.

that we are to think of the humanistic cursive in its altered status, but as an equal in birth; and to the situation, Dr. Lowe's formula is perhaps not to be too rigorously applied.

Sanvito's script had won acceptance, with all its imperfections on its head. These were indeed part of its charm. Its rhythms are agreeably varied; its asymmetries—the token of sensibility rather than of failure—pleasing. His italic script is true to its nature: it remains informal. But in the process of its elevation to the status of a book-hand, italic could not, for obvious reasons, continue so. In the hands of highly skilled professionals like Pierantonio Sallando, some time *lector ad artem scribendi* in the University of Bologna,[1] the script became subject to the operations of discipline, organization and rationalization which the professional in any art will bring to his material. If we look again at the manuscript of Alberti's architecture which Sallando wrote at Padua in 1483 for the dying Duke of Urbino [40], we shall see the formalizing influence at work: witness the consistent pattern; the uniformity of slope; the sedulously articulated serif formation; the lateral compression and 'point'. Sallando's script is on the whole reticent; controlled; correct. But the new field of scribal activity had room also for the more obvious calligraphic qualities of abandon and exuberance, even in places where a decent reverence might seem to have precluded its use. Additional MS. 22805 has many points of interest, not least among them the circumstances of its making [41]. It commemorates Orsino Lanfredini, the son of Giovanni Lanfredini, Florentine Ambassador to the court of Pope Innocent VIII.[2] The youth, comely in person and rich in intellectual promise, was the hope and pride of his father; but he kept bad company, and his end in 1488 is Shakespearian in its poignancy, recalling as it does the scene in *Romeo and Juliet* where Tibalt dies. Orsino Lanfredini, never to enjoy the lucrative benefice that Pope Innocent had destined for his majority,[3] fell in a street brawl between the rival factions of Orsini and Cibò, aged eighteen years. The fatality was deplored in a sequence of elegies composed by the most eminent latinists of the age, including Politian and Bernardino Capella. Those the sorrowing family caused to be collected

---

[1] See J. Wardrop, 'Pierantonio Sallando and Girolamo Pagliarolo', in *Signature* N.S. ii, 1946, pp. 4–30.

[2] For the Lanfredini see M. Mansfield, *A Family of Decent Folk (1200–1741)*, &c., Florence, 1922.

[3] Grand Priorate of Capua in the Order of St. John of Jerusalem.

into a book which, bearing the Lanfredini arms, was written under the editorship of Vasino Gambara,[1] presumably soon after the event, by an unknown scribe, in gold upon black vellum which has not withstood the darkening agent: the little manuscript is now in a fragmentary state, preserved between sheets of gauze.

The script, which can with reasonable certainty be assigned to the year 1489, was probably written at Rome, where the Lanfredini tragedy occurred. It has the characteristic admixture of majuscule forms, Venetian in origin as we have suggested; but its palaeographical interest lies in the treatment of the ascenders. These, instead of being seriffed as in the script of Sanvito or Sallando, are (to use a typographer's term) kerned: that is to say they terminate, not in a bracket attached to the left of the shaft, but in a turn (an *Abschwung* as German palaeographers say) to the right, crowned with a tiny point. This mode, standard in the sixteenth century, begins to make its appearance, as far as my observation goes, in the last decade of the fifteenth; but it would be a useful work on the part of some advanced student of palaeography, by close analysis and comparison, to determine precisely when and where it was introduced; for its incidence marks the beginning of the 'modern' era in writing. Notice that in the specimen illustrated, the descenders still retain the serif, which in the sixteenth century are brought into conformity with the ascenders. Notice also the persistence of looped *g*, which, twenty years later, would have been regarded as a solecism, in apposition to a kerned ascender.

A further stage in the formalization of italic script is seen in Additional MS. 16439 [42]. Though not the work of a first-rate scribe, it strikingly anticipates the calligraphic methods of a later generation. Written at Venice in 1497 by Albertus Mapheanus, the manuscript contains the pastoral poem *Cephalo e l'aurora* of Niccolò da Coreggio, some time court poet to the Este family at Ferrara;[2] and bears the arms of Belegno, together with the unidentified initials J. A., and the subscription S.P.Q.V.—Senatus Populusque Venetus. It will be noticed that the writing lacks that element which Mr. Hewitt judged to be the basis of a true cursive—a systematic running line[3]—

---

[1] Nephew of Bernardino Gambara; *cubicularius secretus*, 1490; solicitor, 1493; subdeacon apostolic, 1495; †1501. See M. Bertola, *I due primi registri di prestito della Biblioteca Apostolica Vaticana*, Città del Vaticano, 1942, p. 24.

[2] See A. Arata, *Niccolò da Coreggio*, Bologna, 1934.

[3] *Handwriting*, London, 1938, p. 96.

but is rather built up in a series of discrete strokes which give a solid archi-tectural quality to the page, not out of keeping with its general design, but little consonant with the original intention of the script. It is fairly obvious that we are, in 1497, already in the presence of italic writing constructed according to rule; and in which the principles of geometry (that *Fata Morgana* of the sixteenth-century theorists) are at least implied.

From 1480 onwards, an increasing number of books, classical as well as vernacular texts, were written in the humanistic cursive or italic; and by 1500 it had, effectively, displaced the *antica* or roman. It became difficult to find scribes who could write *antica* well, that is as Contugi and Mennio had done in their prime. Two interdependent factors were responsible for this: the spread of printing and the decline of patronage. The press in Italy had appropriated the *antica* to its uses in 1465; and by the end of the century, to quote Mr. Scholderer 'no new book of any quality was likely to fail of the permanence conferred by print'.[1] There is no need to point the analogy: the texts of the major classics had all been printed. It is clear that by the eighties the economic situation of the professional copyist must have gravely deteriorated. We know so little of the actual conditions under which Renais-sance scribes worked, that it is impossible to be precise. They are as a rule obstinately silent about themselves. It is only through chance survivals—such as the letters of Matteo Contugi[2] and the diary of Bartolomeo Sanvito[3]—that we are vouchsafed a glimpse into their lives. In a document preserved in the Archivio Civico at Padua, dated 1471,[4] the copyist and miniaturist Giovanni Martinengo complains bitterly of lack of work, saying that he envies the lot of a beggar, and threatens to remove himself to Venice, with his wife and six children: Marcello, Elisio, Catelina, Grandizia, Bernardina, and Petronella. Certainly the press broke up the great *scriptoria* and set their fellowship upon the road. The last quarter of the century witnessed the emergence of the freelance, and often peripatetic, scribe. In Martinengo's predicament, many a man has found consolation in the thought that if the worst comes to the worst there's always teaching. So the displaced copyist would establish himself, hoping for the best, in some town or village, and there announce his readiness to give instruction in writing and arithmetic.

---

[1] *Printers and Readers in Italy in the Fifteenth Century* (Annual Italian lecture of the British Academy), London, 1949, p. 23.

[2] See *supra*, pp. 9–10.

[3] See *supra*, p. 26.

[4] Estimo 1418, Tomo 146, Polizze 41, 43, 44.

His credentials might take the form of a specimen-book, or simply a little strip of vellum or paper bearing an alphabet or an appropriate legend in his best hand. Examples of these single leaves are extremely rare. One was found a year or so ago between the pages of an incunable in the Library of the Brompton Oratory, by the then Librarian, Father Patrick Bushell. It is the *proba* of a certain Giovanbattista [43], who unfortunately does not tell us his surname, but who describes himself as master of arithmetic and writing to the community of Volterra. I judge the piece to be of the period 1480–90.

Towards the end of the fifteenth century the tradition of writing had begun to pass more and more into the hands of the pedagogue; and with the sixteenth century, the dawn of modern times, the tradition merges with the common business of mankind. The script of humanism was becoming, in Mr. Hewitt's phrase 'Everyman's craft'. But before we turn to a brief review of the Italian writing-masters who conveyed the script to us, it concerns us as palaeographers to trace the sources of their inspiration; to determine, if we can, how the humanistic cursive became, as we said, the medium of polite correspondence, not only within the Italian peninsula, but throughout most of Europe. It is a task calling for assiduity, prudence and tact, and one which must extend beyond the pages of this work.

The Italian writing-masters, from Tagliente and Arrighi to Scalzini and beyond, refer to the cursive hand which they practised and inculcated, as *cancellaresca corsiva* or *lettera da brevi*: chancery cursive, or brief script. The nomenclature tells us much; but not enough to have prevented a good deal of confusion. Chancery script is, by definition, the writing, not necessarily humanistic, or cursive, used in a chancery, any chancery.[1] A chancery, for the purposes of this inquiry, is that department or office of an administrative or legislative body, concerned with the dispatch, and to some extent also with the receipt and filing, of letters. In Renaissance times it might be said, in Civil Service parlance, to have combined the functions of a correspondence section and a registry. There were chanceries all over Italy—at Venice, Ferrara, Naples, Bologna, and, *a fortiori*, at Rome, all emitting letters. A brief is a special kind of papal letter, whose origin has been traced to the pontificate of Boniface IX (1389–1404).[2] In 1522 papal briefs were

---

[1] For chancery scripts in the wider sense, see V. Federici, *La scrittura delle cancellerie italiane dei sec. XII–XVII*, Roma, 1934.

[2] Cf. K. A. Fink, 'Untersuchungen über die päpstlichen Breven des 15. Jahrhunderts', in *Römische Quartalschrift*, xliii. 1–2, Rom, 1935, pp. 55–86.

being written, in common with the then established usage of other chanceries, in a variant of the humanistic cursive or italic, hence the name chancery cursive. I mention the date 1522, because in that year it pleased Lodovico Arrighi of Vicenza to publish at Rome, engraved specimens of the script. His influential book, to be referred to later,[1] was the first of its kind to be issued with a propagandist intention, i.e. in the interests of non-professional writers. On the title-page he describes himself as *scrittore di brevi apostolici*, writer of papal briefs: that is to say, he was then an employee, one among many, of the papal chancery. Present-day interest in Arrighi's calligraphic models dates from 1926, when Mr. Stanley Morison and the late Frederic Warde, with no thought of the dragons' teeth they were sowing, issued their admirable and exquisitely printed facsimile.[2] Since then public interest in the scripts which Arrighi's example inspired in his own century has noticeably increased, both in England and in the United States. The vogue has given rise to some odd misconceptions. The most egregious of these—that the chancery cursive was the invention, either in name or in practice, of Arrighi—surely concerns no discerning student. The still prevalent notion that it was the exclusive creation of the Roman Curia, or was adopted at the *fiat* of Eugenius IV,[3] merits our further notice, and perhaps a word in modification. A word here and there has been said; but apparently unheard in places where the terms 'chancery' and 'italic' and 'humanistic cursive' are most frequently and light-heartedly employed. It is obviously of the utmost importance for us to know when, and where, and in what circumstances the humanistic cursive was gathered into the diplomatic fold. In considering this aspect of the problem, we must perpend most carefully what we are entitled to say. No document, no *motus proprius* of Eugenius IV (1431–47) authorizing or specifically assigning the humanistic cursive to the use of the papal chancery has been found; and since no brief in the humanistic *cursive* (cursive is here the operative word) dating from his pontificate has been observed, it is doubtful if the elusive instrument will ever turn up. The briefs of Eugenius IV are in fact written in the formal *antica*; an important point, but not the one for which we are contending. It was under Pius II (1458–64) that the practice of inditing briefs in the

---

[1] See *infra*, p. 45.

[2] *The calligraphic models of Ludovico degli Arrighi surnamed Vicentino*, Paris (privately printed), 1926.

[3] The belief seems to rest on the *ipse dixit* of J. M. J. L. de Mas Latrie, *Trésor de chronologie,* &c., Paris, 1889, coll. 1136, 1137.

cursive hand appears to have been established. Thenceforward it becomes a recognized convention.

So far, the evidence for the use of the humanistic cursive in the papal *brief* is unfavourable to Eugenius IV, if not conclusively against him. On the other hand, one of the earliest 'italics' known to me, with all the stylistic and structural features peculiar to that, and in an unquestionably diplomatic context, belongs to the reign of the great humanist pope. It is a privilege granted to the Church of San Giorgio in Alga, Venice, dated from Rome, July the 19th, 1444 [44], the sole survivor of the photographs I had made in 1937 from the *Archivio della Cancelleria della Nunziatura Veneta*, in the Archivio Segreto of the Vatican. Though this act was not necessarily drawn up in the chancery, it none the less shows the assignment of the humanistic cursive to an expressly curial purpose. Indeed it would be surprising if, from the vast documentary legacy of Eugenius, some such token were to be absent. Eugenius IV (Gabriel Condulmer or Condulmieri) was a Venetian, a scholar and the friend of scholars, who had given practical encouragement to that tireless traveller and antiquary, Ciriaco of Ancona; whose domestic prelacy was composed, not unnaturally, of men from his own region; and with whom he may be thought to have shared the calligraphic interests which flourished there. But the point of precedence—which of the chanceries, Venice, Rome, Ferrara, Bologna, Naples, was the first to adopt the humanistic cursive for its official missives—can only be settled when the archives of those cities have been palaeographically examined, and in the utmost detail. It is an urgent challenge to which advanced students of palaeography might take heed. In the case of Naples it is already too late.

To sum up, what are we justified, by the evidence, in saying of Rome, and of Lodovico Arrighi? Surely this: that it was the destiny of Rome to modify, to chasten and bend to her will, a form of writing which enjoyed a lively existence in other centres and whose influence was simultaneously exerted, and in varying degree received, throughout Italy. Further: it was Rome's part to set upon the humanistic cursive—as it is her wont to do on all her property—an indelible stamp; and, by discouraging calligraphic excess, to preserve as it were an adopted child in the path of virtue. Again, to Rome belongs at least half the credit for the diffusion throughout Christendom, of the humanistic cursive by means of the papal brief. Lastly, it was Arrighi's part to confer upon the script the permanence and the ubiquity of print.

The *lettera da brevi* was brought to maturity and (typographically speaking) acquired its characteristically 'italic' cast, during the pontificates of Leo X and his immediate successors, Hadrian VI and Clement VII. It was in Leo's time (1513–21) that papal scriptors caught the habit of over-compression and angularity in their writing, which was to become a progressively vitiating influence upon the cursive hand. In effect that was often very beautiful, as the illustration, part of a brief of Clement VII, testifies [45]. Nor was the habit necessarily due to caprice. There was, as in the thirteenth century, an economic reason for space-saving. Vellum, never abundant or cheap, was again becoming scarce and expensive—particularly in the high qualities which the Vatican preferred—and a writer of briefs had to condense his matter into a sheet measuring some 17 by 5 inches. Making a virtue of necessity, scribes carried the practice into the manuscript book, where space-saving is not a primary consideration. But by the early sixteenth century the *scriptor librarius* was fast disappearing; and there were few institutions which could offer full-time employment to men whose only virtue lay in their pens. *Caeteris paribus*, good penmanship was still a prime recommendation to vacancies in the papal secretariat; and once there, a man might go far. The Vatican was the goal of poets and *prosateurs* and social aspirants; just as here, in other days, it used to be the custom of mildly literary young men to attach themselves to some government department, as an appropriate background for their talents, and to help provide for the day that was passing over them. The phenomenon, in Renaissance times, is strikingly illustrated by the brilliant, and largely scandalous career of Evangelista Maddaleni, known for literary convenience as Fausto Capodiferro.[1]

Fausto Capodiferro was poet and papal scriptor like his friend Marcantonio Casanova, whose melancholy fate he shared in the disaster of 1527. A pupil of Pomponio Leto, he lived to fill, with no great applause, the chair of history at the Sapienza in 1514; but he was perhaps even more at home in the tavern or the boudoir. He figures in the famous dialogue between

[1] Cf. especially O. Tommasini, 'Evangelista Maddaleni de' Capodiferro accademico', &c., in *Atti della R. Accademia dei Lincei*, 4th ser., x, Roma, 1892, pp. 3–20. See also H. Janitschek, in *Repertorium für Kunstwissenschaft*, iii, Berlin, 1880, pp. 52–60; V. Cian, in *Giornale storico della letteratura italiana*, xxix, Torino, 1897, pp. 443–4, 449[1]; E. Steinmann, *Die Sixtinische Kapelle*, ii, München, 1905, pp. 6[1], 164[4], 59[1]; A. Campana, in *Maso Finiguerra*, xiv–xv, fasc. 2–3, Milano, 1936, p. 167; M. Bellonci, *Lucrezia Borgia*, 3rd ed., Milano, 1939, *passim*.

[2] See *Philippi Beroaldi Junioris carminum*, &c., Romae (A. Bladus), 1530.

Filippo Beroaldo Junior and the courtesan Imperia,[2] as the donor of a silver necklace—*argentea lunula*—to that accommodating but rapacious beauty. 'Strenuus compotor, neque scortator ignavus'—Erasmus's words would fit him: venal and lascivious, says Tomassini. Capodiferro was a partisan of the Colonna, and passed for a friend of the Borgia; that is to say, he was the most patent type of sycophant or *cliens*; one of those (and they are still with us) who, quick to sneer at Trimalchio behind his back, are usually to be found at his table. But Fausto was a poet of the highest technical accomplishment; a passable musician and an amusing fellow to whom, doubtless for all three reasons, Alexander Borgia gave a measure of latitude large even for the most tolerant of pontiffs. When Bernard of Montefalco, papal scriptor, complained to His Holiness of the abduction of his daughter by Capodiferro, 'Papa' says the chronicle 'subrisit'.[1] He would have smiled, as the vulgarism is, on the other side of his face, if he could have seen the poet's commonplace-book[2] where, side by side with the adulatory verses already known to the Pope, there were inserted others in which the persons of himself and his family were ridiculed, and their vices stigmatized, with a venom, and in language, worthy of Martial.[3] Capodiferro admired, and in some ways resembled, the caustic little Aragonese; but whereas Martial knew pity, even tenderness, Fausto's heart was as hard as his head. His epigrams have an undercurrent of sheer nastiness, and a depth of cynicism which go far to explain, in what they reveal of humanism corrupted, the causes of the Sack of Rome. Fate, which spared their author the poisoned cup, reserved him for the Landsknechts.

Vaticano Latino 10377 is the manuscript of Capodiferro's verses which the poet wrote in his own hand for presentation to Clement VII [46]; though, as the volume is incomplete, it does not appear that the gift was ever received.[4] The first page is on purple vellum, with the text in silver and gold. The script is closely related to the *lettera da brevi* as seen in the brief of Clement VII [45], and is doubtless little different from the writing which the author used in his official capacity at the chancery. It was manuscripts of this class that the saturnine and terrible Lutheran, Sebastian Schertlin von Burtenbach, tore up with such satanic and boastful zest in 1527.[5]

---

[1] See Tommasini, loc. cit.

[2] MS. Vat. Lat. 3351.

[3] e.g. the lines on Sperata Coppi, quoted by Tommasini, loc. cit.

[4] See M. Vattasso and E. Carusi, *Codices Vaticani latini*, &c., Romae, 1920.

[5] See his autobiography, quoted by L. Pastor, *History of the Popes*, ix, London, 1910, p. 414.

Printing, which killed writing as a trade, favoured its development as an art. In accordance with our terms of reference it remains for us to say a word on the succession of the great Italian writing-masters. At their head stands another victim of the Sack of Rome, Lodovico Arrighi, called Vicentino, papal scriptor, *scriptor librarius* and printer.[1] His fame in modern times owes almost everything to Mr. Morison, who built around him a classic chapter in typographical history. First known as a publisher at Corneto Tarquinia in 1510, Arrighi himself made history by publishing at Rome in 1522 his modest but revolutionary *Operina*,[2] from which, by the means of engraved models of the script, the public was optimistically invited to learn, in a few days, how to write *cancellaresca*, that blessed word [47]. Arrighi's script deserves every jot of its renown; for, free as it is of affectation or archaism, it has a timeless grace and charm, to which no successor attained. Of his current *lettera da brevi*, no holograph specimen has been traced; but to his formal italic book-hand there are impressive witnesses: first, the Latin Aristotle [48], now in the University Library, Amsterdam, which he wrote for Vittoria Colonna in 1517;[3] and secondly, of the same year, the list of benefactors of the hospital of San Giovanni in Laterano, better known to the Roman, in the pronunciation of his classical ancestors, as the Salvatore 'ad Santa Santorm' [49].[4]

Arrighi's pioneer venture of 1522 was followed up, two years later, by the *Presente Libro* of the Venetian, Giovanantonio Tagliente [51a & b].[5] Though forestalled in the market by Arrighi, Tagliente was old in years and experience when he published, having held, since 1492, under privilege of the Senate, the office of writing-master to the Venetian Chancery. It is even possible that Arrighi, born in the neighbouring town of Vicenza, may have been one of his pupils. Tagliente's work bears all the marks of the elder generation to which he belonged; and his script, full of archaisms and other

---

[1] For an account (with bibliography) of Arrighi as scribe and printer, see J. Wardrop, 'Arrighi revived', in *Signature*, xii, London, 1939, pp. 26–46.

[2] *La operina di Ludovico Vicentino, da imparare di scrivere littera cancellarescha.*

[3] M.S. II.A.19.

[4] Rome, Archivio di Stato, MS. 1010 (unsigned: the attribution is mine). For a description of this book and a coloured reproduction of a page, see O. Montenovesi, in *Accademie e biblio-*teche d'Italia, anno XVI, fasc. v, Roma, 1942, pp. 282–7. I am disposed to ascribe also to the hand of Arrighi an Horae in the Fitzwilliam Museum (M. R. James no. 156); and a MS. of Vartema's travels now in the Biblioteca Nazionale, Florence, for which see A. Mondolfo, in *Studi di bibliografia . . . in memoria di L. de Gregori*, Roma, 1949, pl. XIII.

[5] See J. Wardrop, 'A note on Giovanantonio Tagliente', in *Signature*, N.S. viii, 1949, pp. 57–61.

traps for the unwary, harks back to the exuberant patterns of Ciriaco and Feliciano. A special interest attaches to the unique document, from the Archivio di Stato in Venice [50].[1] It is the original holograph supplication addressed in 1491 by Tagliente to the Doge and the Council of Ten, in which, to quote the calligrapher's own words, he 'offers himself to teach and instruct chancery writing with its rules to all the young men dedicated to Your Excellency's Chancery'. The request, incredible as it may seem, was at first turned down; but Tagliente secured the post a year later, by the exercise of some interest; much ingenuity; and even a little of what I learned in America to call 'chiselling'. But there can be no doubt that for the Council of Ten it was a most prudent and profitable appointment.

It was more than fifteen years before another 'chancery' manual of any importance appeared in Italy. The Sack of Rome, so sudden in its impact, so terrible in its consequences, had intervened. Thereafter nothing was as it had been. The cold wind of the Counter-reform blew on literature and art alike. Yet there was nothing cold in the temperament, or in the art, of Giovanbattista Palatino,[2] the calligraphic prodigy from Calabria, who published his *Libro nuovo d'imparare a scrivere* at Rome in 1540. Palatino, the most versatile and popular of all the Italian writing-masters, was a prominent figure in the intellectual society of the Capital. Founder, along with Tomasso Spica and Girolamo Ruscelli, of the Academy of the *Sdegno* or *Sdegnati*, he consorted there on equal terms with Cardinal Alessandro Farnese; Claudio Tolomei; Francesco Maria Molza; Giulio Clovio and others; and once, as Secretary of the Academy, welcomed to the assembled company, in a passionate speech, the reigning beauty, Faustina Mancini. He was the first of the writing-masters to give us his portrait; and to that he added his handsome academic device of the moth and lighted candle. His writing-book, published in three versions and in numerous editions [52], had an immense, but transient vogue; and he might claim to have influenced, not necessarily for the better, the handwriting of half Europe. The direct evidences of his skill are to be found in two manuscripts, conserved respectively in the Bodleian Library and the University of Tübingen. The first, Canonici MS. Ital. 196, conveniently illustrates the features of his chancery style. It will be noticed that in this script, the faults of over-compression and

[1] Cons. X, Misti, filza 5, f. 127.
[2] See J. Wardrop, 'Civis romanus sum: Giovanbattista Palatino and his circle', in *Signature*, N.S. xiv, 1952, pp. 3–38.

angularity, already referred to, are pushed to the extreme; and that a true cursive movement is absent [53]. The constituent strokes are fitted together rather than welded or fused; and though this is done with the utmost adroitness, the method smacks more of draughtsmanship than of penmanship. There can be little doubt that Palatino wrote rapidly, and to see him in action must have been a spectacle; but one cannot escape the feeling that he set an impossible standard; and whilst it is all very well for Palatino, it is not so well for you or me. That view was held by at least one contemporary. The *reductio ad absurdum* of this method was reached by Ferdinando Ruano, a Spaniard from the diocese of Badajoz, latin *scriptor* of the Vatican Library from 1541 to 1560.[1] In 1553 Ruano published his *Sette alphabeti*, in which he perversely sponsored the construction of chancery letters according to the rules of geometry [54]. It is a matter for relief, though not for surprise, that his book had no influence whatsoever. But it would be misleading, and unjust to Ruano, to dismiss him without some earnest of his real competence. That is to be found, for example, in the Hildibertus (MS. Vaticano Latino 3841) which he wrote in *cancellaresca formata* script for Julius III in 1551 [55].

Palatino's script, manifestly unsuited to the needs of ordinary mortals, was certain to provoke reaction. Already in 1554 the Franciscan, Vespasiano Amphiareo or Albertacci, was offering at Venice calligraphic models which combined with the rigid and over-disciplined strokes of the gothicizing Palatino, some of the aids to currency—such as loops and running ligatures —found in contemporary mercantile hands. The illustration from Vespasiano's engraved manual [56] shows the innovation which the Friar does not scruple to advertise as *bastarda*, and to claim that he has invented.

But the most decisive and violent reactionary against the authority of Palatino was the Milanese, Gianfrancesco Cresci,[1] appointed *scriptor* to the Vatican Library in 1556, and to the Sistine Chapel in 1558: that is to say, just about the time when the masses of Palestrina were first heard in that sanctuary. Cresci was a skilled penman, and a very considerable artist. Despite a choleric temper, he had a clear and logical mind, which he exercised upon the craft of writing, on the whole always in the direction of common sense and rationalization. The academic preoccupations of Palatino and his friends—wistfully bent on prolonging an artistic interval—seemed

[1] See J. Wardrop 'The Vatican Scriptors: Documents for Ruano and Cresci', in *Signature*, N.S. V, 1948, pp. 3–28.

to him to be mere unmanly fribbling. Leo X was a memory; Paul III was in his grave, and there was no more time to play. Palatino's script could not stand the strain of business, therefore away with it. Overboard with geometry; overboard with edged pens: let us be back to handwriting, handwriting that flows. Such would seem to have been Cresci's cry; and I dare say it might find an echo in some hearts today. Certainly Cresci would have agreed to the proposition that there is a fundamental disparity in the intention, and the means, of one who would write the Book of Kells, and one who would write a civil letter to a friend. Cresci's views, and his specimens, are embodied in the now rare little book *Essemplare*, which appeared at Rome in 1560 [57]. It was destined to be the last great formative influence on European handwriting. Changes of taste are simultaneously manifested in all the arts: rationalist though he was, Cresci belonged to the age of the *baroque*, and his script carries its characteristic impress. The tiny point, which initiates a kerned ascender, had by Cresci's time been magnified to the dimensions of a crowning feature, soon to become standard, well into the seventeenth century, as *cancellaresca testeggiata*. Its effect in mass is sometimes quite splendid, as is seen in the letter written by Cresci to his protector, Cardinal Sirleto, in 1572 [58]. It is not difficult to detect, in its contours and flourishes, the prefiguration of Victorian copperplate: less easy, perhaps, to evoke from them the serene and comely form, 'noble and nude and antique' in Swinburne's words, 'castigata et clara' in Petrarch's, that the Tuscan saw in the pages of Horace.

With Cresci we reach the stipulated limit of our survey. Of the vast territory comprehended, it has been at most a Pisgah sight. In the space at our disposal we have been able only to select a standpoint—not necessarily the best—and from our distant station to mark, here a hilltop, there a valley or a stream.

When I first embarked on this study I chose for it a title which would give me the utmost latitude. Of that latitude I have perhaps too freely availed myself: I may even have abused it by posing more questions than I have been able to answer; or worse still, by falling, the moment after, into some error I have presumed to reprehend. Less vaguely, and perhaps with greater relevance, I might have named my series 'Script as an aspect of humanism'. The designation would have expressed more accurately my general intention; and it is in such a light—if light there has been—that I should wish advanced students of palaeography to ponder the subject.

The illustrations, for the most part drawn from manuscripts studied by me when I was working as a Leverhulme Research Fellow in 1947 to 1949, are to be regarded merely as *documents pour servir*: that they should serve also *pour encourager les autres* is my pious hope.

In conclusion may I venture to ask advanced students of palaeography to do two things: first, to be unremitting in the search for original documentary sources; and to preserve always a polite but profound scepticism in the face of any unqualified statement that does not rest on their authority. Remember Fustel de Coulanges: '*Avez-vous un texte?*' I do not go so far as to say that documents cannot mislead or lie; but they do not mislead or lie half so often as the printed word; and the axiom that one page of contemporary evidence is worth a chapter of latter-day criticism will not generally be found fallacious. 'Verify your references' is an old and wise counsel: it is necessary to do more than that, to verify other people's references. It is always an instructive, sometimes a chastening, experience.

Further, may I exhort the advanced student of palaeography to add, if he has not already done so, to the knowledge of Latin and Greek, which are the parole of the learned everywhere, a thorough knowledge of the Italian language. The acquisition, if not a *sine qua non*, will be found no impediment to palaeographical studies. It may not be inappropriate to end with a quotation: the words of a poet who is the ornament of two literatures, our beloved John Florio. The lines are from the sonnet which he wrote, in a hand worthy of a humanist, in the copy of his Dictionary which he presented in 1598 to Sir Thomas Egerton, then Lord Keeper of the Seal to Elizabeth the First:

> *Cato in yeares learn't Greeke, for Romanes weare*
> *To deale with Grecians, and in Greeke was writt*
> *Philosophie of nature, manners, witt:*
> *Which grace to him, good to his Rome might reare.*
> *Owr English Cato then (who manie a yeare*
> *Censorious maie in vertues Senate sitt)*
> *It maie without disparagement befitt*
> *To knowe Italiane; since Italianes beare*
> *Inteligence with moste, and writing showe*
> *What Greece, or Rome, ages or places knewe:*

. . . .

Manuscripts by Bartolomeo Sanvito of Padua

CAMBRIDGE

King's College   MS. 34   Horace

CAMBRIDGE MASS.

Harvard University Library   Sallust   See Sotheby's Catalogue, 9 May 1933.

CHATSWORTH

Duke of Devonshire   *Silloge* of Fra Giocondo   See R. A. Lanciani, *Storia degli scavi di Roma*, i, 1902, pp. 96–100.

ETON

Eton College Library   MS. 149   Cicero, *De Officiis*   Signed with initials. *See* Burlington Fine Arts Club, *Catalogue of an Exhibition of Illuminated MSS.*, 1908.

FLORENCE

Biblioteca Laurenziana   Plut. 53 . 2   Calderini, *Commentary* on Juvenal

LEEDS

Brotherton Collection   Juvenal

LONDON

British Museum

Royal 14. C 3	Eusebius, *Chronica*	Illuminated by Giulio Clovio *c.* 1540, but written by B.S.
King's 24	Virgil	
Stowe 1016	*Silloge* of Fra Giocondo	
Add. 20927	Horae (Stewart de Rothesay)	
Harley 2528	Valerius Probus	
Harley 3567	Petrarch	Written and signed by Matteo Contugi for a bishop of the Gonzaga family whose arms are featured. An index of first lines has been supplied in another hand, apparently the roman script of B.S.; there is, moreover, an interlinear commentary, as far as f. 22 in a cursive almost undoubtedly by him. The miniatures and decoration are apparently related to MS. Bod. Canon. Ital. 85 which also has the Gonzaga arms.
Harley 2692	Cicero, *De officiis*	Signed in initials and dated 23 October 1498. Almost identical with Eton Cicero (*see below*).
Harley 6051	Cicero, *De officiis*	Date (erased) presumably 1494.
	Dictys Cretensis	
	Petrarch	
	Petrarch	

Chester Beatty Collection

Harvey Frost Collection

Victoria and Albert Museum — Formerly in the Holford Collection.

MADRID

Biblioteca Nacional

| | *Silloge* of Fra Giocondo | |
| | Eusebius, *Chronica* | See J. Domínguez Bordona, *Manuscritos con pinturas.* |

MONSELICE (near Padua)

Collegiate Church of Santa Giustina

Epistolary ⎱
Evangelary ⎰ — Signed in initials and dated 1509.

NEW YORK

Public Library — Lectionary
Private Collection — Martial — Sotheby, 7–10 July 1914 Formerly Lewisohn Collection, since sold by Chaucer Head Bookshop, New York to a private collector. See B. Quaritch, *Examples of Book Illumination*, i, 1889, Pl. xii; Hoe Sale Catalogue, New York, 1911, i, n. 2149.

OXFORD

Bodleian Library — Martial — Auct. F. 4. 33 — See *Italian Illuminated Manuscripts*, (Exhibition Catalogue), 1948 (21).

PADUA

Museo Civico — Inventory of B.S.'s property — Estimo 1418, Tom. 245, Polizza 53

PRINCETON N.J.

Princeton University — Virgil — VRG MS. 2945/1400

RAVENNA

Biblioteca Classense — Horae — See D. Fava, *Tesori delle biblioteche d'Italia*, 1932, p. 241.
*Petrarch
*Cicero
*Horae

ROME

Vatican Library — Homer in Greek and Latin — Vat. Grec. 1626 — Bears arms of Cardinal Francesco Gonzaga. Greek text finished by Giovanni Rossos in 1477.

Vatican Library — *Silloge* of Fra Giocondo — Vat. Lat. 10228

STRATHFIELD SAYE (near Silchester)

Duke of Wellington Collection	Suetonius	Containing arms of Ludovico Agneli.

VIENNA

National Bibliothek	Horace	See Hermann, *Beschr. Verzeichnis*, N.F., vi. 4, 1933, pp. 35–37, pl. xi.

WOLFENBÜTTEL

State Library	Alexander Cortesius	See A. de Hevesey, *La Bibliothèque du Roi Matthias Corvin*, Paris, 1923.

This list, compiled from the author's notes, does not include manuscripts attributed since 1952.

★ This indicates that there is a question-mark against the attribution in the author's notes.

INDEX

PLATES

1. Horace acquired by Petrarch in 1347 showing Petrarch's *fere humanistica* or near humanistic note gloss. Florence, Biblioteca Laurentiana, *Plut. 34. 1*

Credo equidem Serenissime princeps qd
tamen pace tua dixerim quia non sic te il
lustrat et in nomen eternum effert militaris
gloria triumphusq. noue gentis conse
crat ut te libelli huius illustrat elegantia
Her Michael de Salvaticis Alemanus
primus huius libri scriptor / ac Incliti se
natus Venetorum notarius Capitum
exteriorum / qui se admodum tue fidei
jurisdictioniq. comendat quem etiam
tua Serenitas iis annume
rare uelit quos sibi maxi
me affectos intel
ligit ⁖
d
va
l
e
⁖
i

2. Michael de Salvaticis: dialogue of Fra Ludovico Strassoldo of Forlì for presentation to the Emperor Sigismond. Rome, Vatican Library, *Vat. Chig. D. VI. 97*

A CAPTIVITATE TROIAE VSQVEADPRIMÃ
OLÝMPIADEM FIVNT AN. CCCC.VI. COLLIGI
TVROMNE TEMPVS, VSQVE IN PRESENTEM
DIEM SECVNDVMASSYRIOS. A XLIIIANNORE
GNI NINI ANNI. DCCCXXXV SECVNDVMHE
BRAEOS A PRIMO ANNO NATIVITATIS ABRA
HAM AN DCCCXXXV SECVNDVMSICYONI
OS A XXII ANNO EVROPIS SIMILITER ANNI
DCCCXXXV A NATIVITATE VERO MOSI ANN.
CCCCX. A PRIMO ANNO CECROPIS QVI PRI
MVS APVD ATTICAM REGNAVIT VSQVE AD
CAPTIVITATEM TROIAE ET VSQVE AD XX
IIIAN. MNEST HEI CVI VS HOMERVS MEMIN
IT COMPVTANTVR AN, CCCLXXV SIMILIT
ER A XXXV AETATIS MOSI FIVT AN. CCCLXXV.

M nestrus moritur in melo regrediens a troia. post quem athenis regnauit
Demophon taris rex aegypti qui ab Homero polibus uocatur maritus AL
chandrae cuius meminit in odyssia dicens post troiae captiuitatem menelau
et Helenam ad eum diuertisse.

3. Unknown Paduan scribe, 1450: Eusebius, *Chronica*. Venice, Biblioteca Marciana, *Class. 9, I*

quoq; uras nescire me fateor dequib; obseruato tam dili

gens tam caura narrat? Hax ne[m]hi erubescendum est

ignorare peregrino. a te uero Praetextate discere nec

cuiem pudeat.   PRAETEXTATVS

vnc Praetextatus non solum tibi inquit Hore cum sis ?

agypto oriundus sed ne nobis quidem quib; origo roma

na est erubescendum puto quaerere quod quru dignum

omnes ueteres putauerut: nam de kalendis nonis &idib;

deq; feriarum uaris obseruationib; innumeros auctores

cura questionis exercuit: &ideo nos que dehis ab omnib;

dicta sunt in unum breuter colligimus: Romulus cu

ingenio acri quidem sed agresta fratum proprii ordinaret

imperii initium cuiusq; mensis exillo sumebat die q[uo] noua

lunam conrigister uideri quia non continuo euenit vt

4. Tophio (in part): Macrobius written in Rome in 1461. Cambridge University Library, *Add. MS. 4095*

153

equtem Añ Exultabunt dõ
mino offa humiliata Añ E xa
udi.   P falmus.
E decet hymnus deus i
fyon et tibi reddetur uo
tum in hierlm. ☐ x audi orati
onem meam ad te omnis caro
ueniet ☐ erba iniquorum ꝓua
luerunt fuper nos: et impietati
bus nris tu propitiaberis. ☐ ea
tus quem elegisti et affumpsisti
inhabitabit in atriis tuis. ☐ e
plebimur in bonis domus tuæ

fanctũ eft templum tuũ mi
rabile in equitate ☐ x audi nos
deus falutaris nr fpes omnium
finium terre et i mari loge ☐ re
parans montes in uirtute tua
accinctus potentia qui cõtur
bas profundum maris fonũ flu
☐tuum et? turbabuntur gẽtes
et timebunt qui hitant terminos
a fignis tuis exitus matutini et
uefpere delectaberis. ☐ ifita
fti terram et inebriafti eam ml̃
tiplicafti locupletare eã ☐ lu

fanctum

5. Pierantonio Sallando: Horae. Formerly in the collection of Sir Sydney Cockerell

aut equa manu discessisset: profecto magna
clades atqɔ calamitas rem. p. oppressisset. Neqɔ
illis qui uictoriam adepti forent: ea uti diutius
licuisset: quin defessis ce exanguibus qui plus pos
set imperium atqɔ libertatem extorqueret. Fue
re tamen extra coniurationem complures qui
ad catilinam initio profecti sunt. Jn his erat ful
uius filius senatoris: quem retractum ex itinere
parens iussit necari. Hisdem temporibus rome
lentulus sicuti catilina preceperat: quoscunqɔ
moribus aut fortuna nouis rebus idoneos crede
bat: aut per se aut per alios sollicitabat. Neqɔ solu
ciues: sed cuiuscunqɔ modi genus hominum qd
tantummodo bello usui foret. Jgitur publio um
breno cuidam negocium dat uti legatos allobro
gum requirat: eosqɔ si posset impellat ad societate
belli: existimans publice priuatimqɔ ere alieno op
pressos: preterea quod natura gens gallica bellico
sa esset: facile eos ad tale consilium adduci posse. Vm
brenus quod in gallia negociatus erat plerisqɔ prin
cipibus ciuitatum notus erat: atqɔ eos nouerat. Jtaqɔ
sine mora ubi primum legatos in foro conspexit: per
cunctatus pauca de statu ciuitatis: ce quasi dolens
eius casum: requirere cepit: quem exitum tantis
malis sperarent. postq illos queri uidet de auaritia
magistratuum: accusare senatum: quod in eo au
xilii nihil esset: miseriis suis mortem remedium ex

6. Cerasius or Ciriago: Sallust written at Florence in 1466. London, British Museum, *Add. MS. 16422*

unde: deinde sunt mentis quoniam ex inde propter cladem corporis sint ex
pulsi. & apparuit quoniam uoluntate & magnitudine fortitudinis ad propria
sunt reuersi. Alij uero tanq̈ nequissimo uiro legis latori nostro derogare con
tendunt: cuius uirtuti tempus quidem illud tam longissimum perhibet testi
monium: de legibus autem loqui ampliori sermone opus non fuit. ipse naq̈
per semetipsas apparuerunt piẽ & uerissimam habentes intentionem: & nõ
ad humanum odium sed ad rerum communionem potius inuitantes: iniqui
tatis inimice: cultricesq̈ iustitie: segnitiem & multas expensas procul abijcien
tes: sufficientiam & amorem laboris erudientes: bellum auaritie causa nesci
entes: fortes autem pro se populos esse preparantes: ad supplicia tribuenda
semper ineuitabiles: uerbis nequaq̈ circumueniri possibiles: preparationes
semper operibus exequentes. Hec enim nos semper opera manifestiora litte
ris exhibemus. Quapropter ego confidens dico quia multarum atq̈ meliorũ
rerum nos potius q̈ alij preceptores sumus. Quid enim intranscensibili pieta
te melius est? Quid iustius q̈ legibus obedire? Quid utilius q̈ in alterutros una
nimes esse? & neq̈ in calamitatibus ab inuicem recedere: neq̈ tempore feli
citatum per iniurias discrepare? Sed in bello quidem mortem contempne
re: in pace uero armis aut agriculture uacare: & semper & ubiq̈ credere de
um respicere & solum omnia gubernare. Hec igitur si quidem apud alios
aut scripta sunt primitus aut seruata: firmiorem debemus nos gratiam illis
tanq̈ eorum facti discipuli: uerum nequaq̈ primitus exuterunt. His precipu
e nos utentes agnoscimur & primam eorum inuentionem nostram fuisse de
claramus. Apiones igitur & Molones & quicunq̈ mendacij derogatione cõ
gaudent: conuicti procul abscedant. Tibi autem ẽ pafrodite ueritatem ma
xime diligenti & per te similia nosse de nostro genere cupiantibus: hic li
bellus conscriptus esse dinoscitur ·F·I·N·I·S·

Explicit liber secundus & ultimus Flauij Iosephi de uetustate iudeor̄. Θ

Anno salutis humane M.CCCC.Lxxviij. & xviij. mensis iunij hoc celeberri
mum opus Florentie consumatum est: die autem ueneris: hora uero diei
xxã. Laus honor: imperium & gloria sit omnipotenti Iesuchristo per in
finita seculorum secula. Amen

OMNIVM RERVM VICISSITV

DO EST ⁖

7. Unknown scribe: Josephus written at Florence in 1478. London, British Museum, *Harl. 3699*

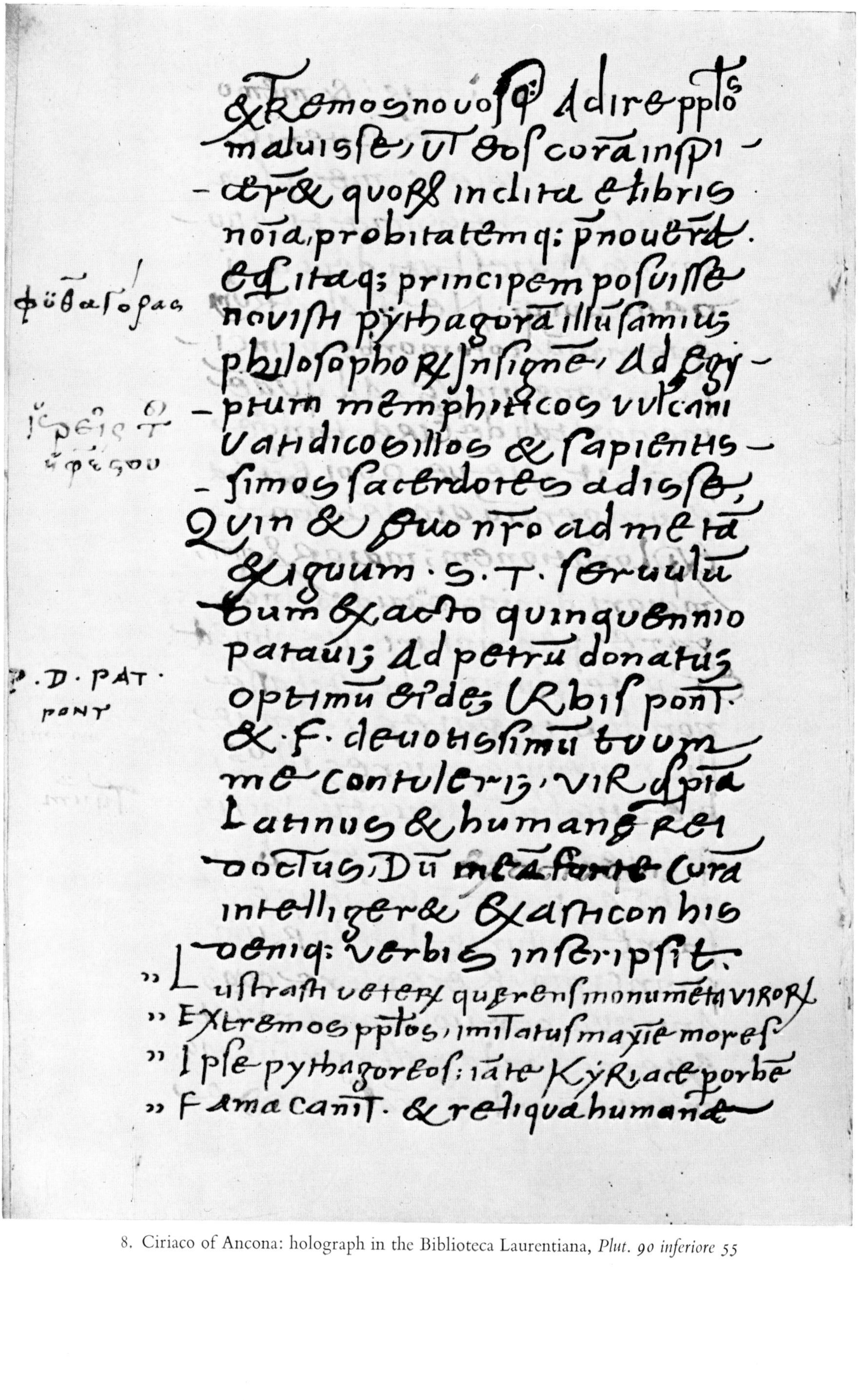

φῦθαγόραϛ

extremos nouosqͫ adireͤ pptͦ
maluisseͤ; ut deos cura inspi -
- cerqͤ quoϠ inclita e libris
no�ią probitatemqͥ pnouerͣt
eϠ itaqͥ principem posuisseͤ
nouisti pythagorͣ illu samiuͥ;
philosophoϠ Insigneͤ; Ad ʒgy -
- ptum memphiticos vulcani
vatidico billos & sapientis -
- simos sacerdotes adisseͤ,
Quin & suo nͬo ad meͤ ta
qͥquum ·s·t· seruulͣ
bum exacto quinquennio
pataui; Ad petru donatuʒ
optimu et des Urbiſ pont·
& f· deuotissimu tuum
meͤ contuleriz; vir dpią
Latinus & humaneͤ rei
doctuʒ; Du mea forte cura
intelligerqͤ exasticon his
deniqͥ: verbiſ inscripsit·
" Lustrasti vetery querenſ monumetͣ viroϠ
" Extremos pptos, imitatuſ maxie moreſ
" Ipse pythagoreoſ; iate Kyriaceͤ porbeͤ
" Fama canit· & reliqua humaneͤ

ἱρεὶϛ θ
ὑρέϛου

?·D·PAT·
PONT

8. Ciriaco of Ancona: holograph in the Biblioteca Laurentiana, *Plut. 90 inferiore* 55

Elegan.ti? Viro.d. Bartholomeo
Aristophilo. Felicianus pauper.

Fami la pouertate. amio mal grado
Ch'io caualco qui in Roma apie per terra
E con putane uechie ognor far guerra
Non esendo perdo ne Eunuco osado
Fami ch dal tonsor piu non mi rado.
Perch nol pago. Sel mio dir non erra
E selo incontro porto el uiso aterra
Per io con questa barba ognor mi uado.
Non e piu vitriol. Ne rocha lume
Ne piu Mercurio nella bocca accesa
Per far lo lapis del philosophastro
Or dunqz uiene ate questo volume
Per carlin diece. da fornir la spesa
Perch non uadi in fumo questo empiastro
    Serai mio bon pilastro
Se mi sostieni chio non cadi al fondo
E tu forse fie lieto e ancor iocundo.

9. Felice Feliciano: letter to Bartolomeo Aristophilo. Rome, Vatican Library, *Vat. Lat. 5641*

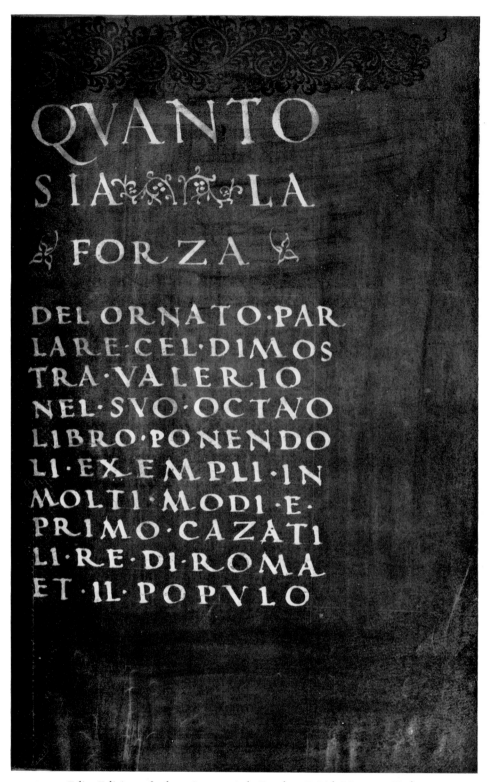

QVANTO
SIA ❧❧❧ LA
❧ FORZA ❧

DEL ORNATO · PAR
LARE · CEL · DI MOS
TRA · VALERIO
NEL · SVO · OCTAO
LIBRO · PONENDO
LI · EXEMPLI · IN
MOLTI · MODI · E ·
PRIMO · CAZATI
LI · RE · DI · ROMA
ET · IL · POPVLO

10. Felice Feliciano: freely written capitals. London, British Museum, *Harl. 5271*

11. Unknown Veronese scribe, fifteenth century, influenced by Felice Feliciano.

12. Frontispiece by Felice Feliciano, 1461. Formerly Holkham MS.

13. Felice Feliciano: page from manuscript written in 1461. Formerly Holkham MS. (from the same MS. as Pl. 12)

14. Pupil of Pomponio Leto: notebook with caricature of master in margin. Rome, Vatican Library, *Vat. Lat.* 3415

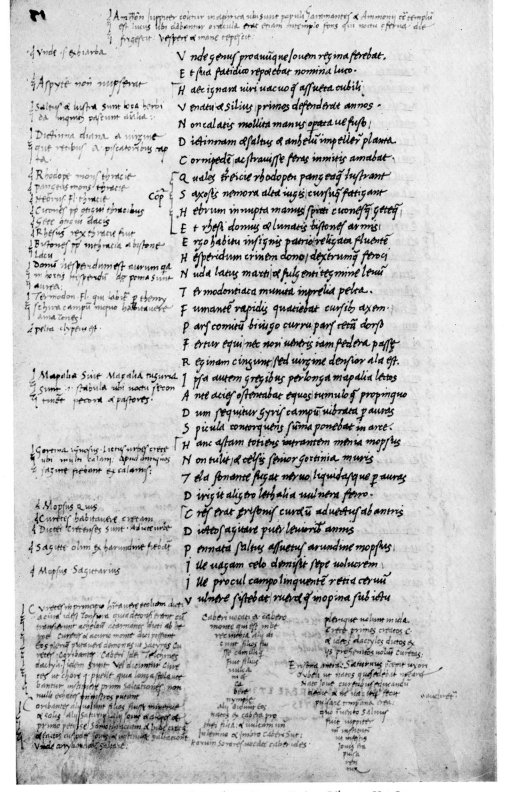

15. Pomponio Leto: Silius Italicus. Rome, Vatican Library, *Vat. Lat. 3302*

ILIADOS·PRIMVS·LIB·HOMERI·CONGLVTINATIONIS

LIB·PRIMVS·PRECES·CHRYSAE·PESTEM·EXERCITVS

ODIVM·REGVM·

RAM CANE DEA PELIDE ACHILLIS
Funestam. quae innumeros achiuis dolores fecit
Multasq; praestantes animas orco misit
Heroum ipsos uero escam fecit canibus
Auibusq, omnibus. iouis aute pficiebatur consiliu
Ex quo primum separati fuerunt litigantes
Atridesq, rex hominum. & diuus achilles
Quisq, ipsos deoz, contentione comouit pugnare
Latonae & iouis filius. ille enim regi iratus
Morbum per exercitum comouit malum. peribant autem populi
Quia chrysen dehonorauit sacerdotem:
Atrides ille enim uenit ueloces ad naues achiuoz,
Redempturusq, filiam ferens innumerabilia munera
Coronamq, tenens in manibus sagittarij apollinis
Aureo in sceptro. & rogabat omnes achiuos
Atridas uero maxime duos duces populoz,
Atrideq, & alij bene ocreati achiui
Vobis quidem dij utinam dent olympias domos colentes
Expugnare priamu urbem bene uero domum redire:
Filiam autem mihi soluite caram munera uero acceptate·
Verentes iouis filium sagitarium apollinem
Tunc alij quidem omnes clamauerunt achiui·

16. Bartolomeo Sanvito: Greek and Latin Homer with arms of Cardinal Francesco Gonzaga. Rome,
Vatican Library, *Vat. Grec. 1626*

TITVS

TITI FLAVII VESPASIA
NI IMPERATORIS VITA
ITVS CO
GNOMI
NE PA
TERNO
AMOR
AC DELICIAE GENERIS

humani tantum illi ad promerendam omnium uolun
tatem, uel ingenij, uel artis, uel fortunæ superfuit. Et
quod difficillimum est in imperio: quando priuatus atq̃,
& sub patre Principe, ne odio quidem nec aum uituperá
tione publica caruit. Natus est iii kl Ian insigni an
no Caiana nece prope septizonium sordidis ædibus, cu
biculo uero perparuo & obscuro. Nam man& adhuc &
ostenditur. Educatus in aula cum Britannico simul
ac paribus disciplinis & apud eosdem magistros institu
tus: quo quidem Tempore aiunt methoposcropum a Nar
ciso Claudij liberto adhibitum ut Britannicum inspi
ceret constantissime affirmasse illum quidem nullo mo
do: Cæter̃ Titum qui prope astabat utiq̃ imperatur̃
Erant autem ita familiares: ut de potione qua Britanni
cus hausta perijt. Titus quoq̃ iuxta cubans gustasse

Septizonium

Methoposcropos

17. Bartolomeo Sanvito: Suetonius written for Ludovico Agneli. The Duke of Wellington
(Strathfield Saye)

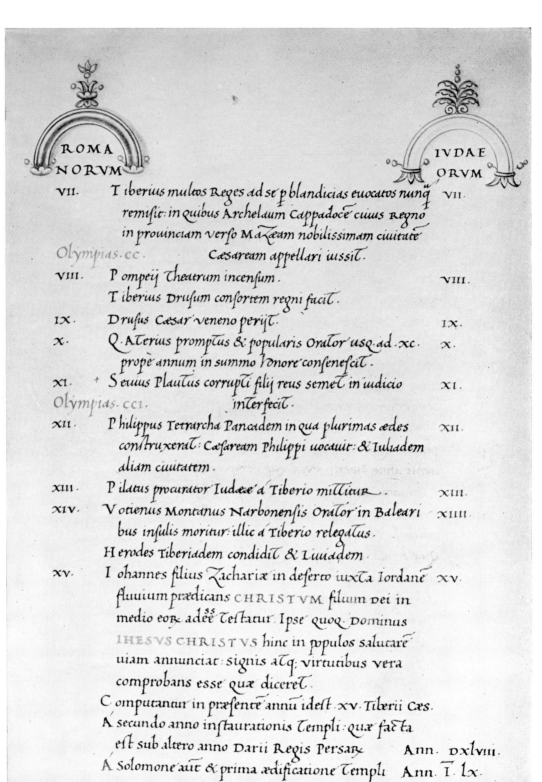

ROMA
NORVM

IVDAE
ORVM

| VII. | Tiberius multos Reges ad se p̄ blandicias euocatos nunq̄ remisit: in quibus Archelaum Cappadoce cuius Regno in prouinciam verso Mazæam nobilissimam ciuitatē Cæsaream appellari iussit. | VII. |

Olympias. cc.

VIII.	Pompeij Theatrum incensum. Tiberius Drusum consortem regni facit.	VIII.
IX.	Drusus Cæsar veneno perijt.	IX.
X.	Q. Aterius promptus & popularis Orator usq. ad .xc. prope annum in summo honore consenescit.	X.
XI.	Seuius Plautus corrupti filij reus semet in iudicio interfecit.	XI.

Olympias. cci.

XII.	Philippus Tetrarcha Pancadem in qua plurimas ædes construxerat: Cæsaream Philippi uocauit: & Iuliadem aliam ciuitatem.	XII.
XIII.	Pilatus procurator Iudææ a Tiberio millitur.	XIII.
XIV.	Votienus Montanus Narbonensis Orator in Baleari bus insulis moritur: illic a Tiberio relegatus. Herodes Tiberiadem condidit & Liuiadem	XIIII.
XV.	Iohannes filius Zachariæ in deserto iuxta Iordanē fluuium prædicans CHRISTVM filium Dei in medio eoꝝ adee Testatur. Ipse quoꝗ Dominus IHESVS CHRISTVS hinc in populos salutare uiam annunciat: signis atꝗ virtutibus vera comprobans esse quæ diceret.	XV.

Computantur in præsente annū idest .xv. Tiberij Cæs.
A secundo anno instaurationis Templi: quæ facta
est sub altero anno Darij Regis Persaꝝ   Ann. Dxlviii.
A Solomone aūt & prima ædificatione Templi   Ann. Ī. lx.

18. Bartolomeo Sanvito: Eusebius written for Bernardo Bembo. London, British Museum, *Royal 14. C. 3*

quod uoluptas condimenti: fortasse no
nihil: utilitatis certe nihil habebit.

Habes a patre munus Marce fili: mea
quidem sententia magnum: sed perin
de erit: ut acceperis. Quanq hi tres
libri inter Cratippi commentarios +
tanq hospites erant excipiendi: Sed
ut si ipse uenissem Athenas: quod
quidem sit factum: nisi me emedio
cursu clara uoce patria reuocasset:
aliquando me quos audires. Sic qua
niam his uoluminibus ad te profecta
uox mea est. Tribue iis temporibus
quantum poteris: poteris autem quam
tum uoles. Cum uero intellexero te
hoc scientiae genere gaudere: Tum
& praesens tecum propediem (ut spe
ro) & dum aberis: absens loquar. Va
le igitur mi Cicero: tibiq; persuade:
te mihi quidem te carissimum: sed
multo fore cariorem: si talibus mo
numentis praeceptisq; laetabere:

M · T · CICERONIS OFFICIORVM
LIB · FINIT · ROMAE DIE
MARTIS · XIV · FEBRVAR,
MCCCCLXXXXVII ,

· B · S ·

(b)

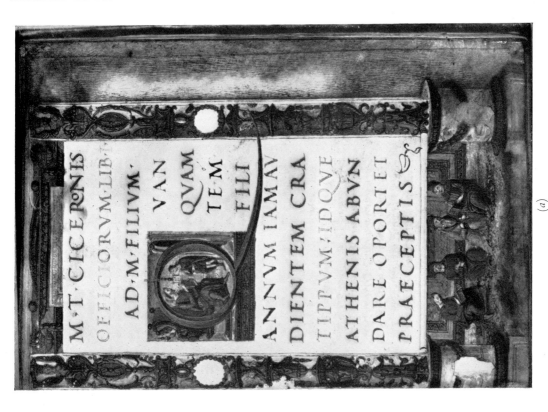

M · T · CICERONIS
OFFICIORVM · LIB ·
AD · M · FILIVM ·

VAN
QVAM
TE · M
FILI

ANNVM IAM AV
DIENTEM CRA
TIPPVM: IDQVE
ATHENIS ABVN
DARE OPORTET
PRAECEPTIS

(a)

19. Bartolomeo Sanvito: Cicero, *De Officiis*, written in Rome, 1497. Library of Eton College, *no. 149.* (*a*) Title-page. (*b*) Colophon with signature

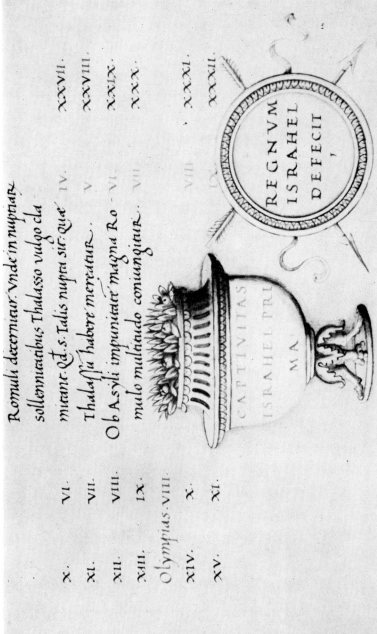

Romuli decernitur. Vnde in nuptias
sollemnitatibus Thalasso vulgo cla-
mitant. Et s. Italis nupta sit. Quæ
Thalasiu habere mercatur.
Ob Asyli impunitate magna Ro-
mulo multitudo coniungitur.

iv.
v.
vi.
vii.

xxvii.
xxviii.
xxix.
xxx.

x.
xi.
xii.
xiii.
Olympias VIII.
x.
xi.

vii.
ix.
xxxi.
xxxii.

CAPTIVITAS
ISRAHEL PRI
MA

REGNVM
ISRAHEL
DEFECIT

Decem Tribus gentes Iudex quæ deficiunt ab Israhel & erant in pace
Samariæ usq; a Senacherib Rege Caldæor. Translatæ sunt in
montes Medor. Regnumq; est in Samaria annis CCL.

20. Bartolomeo Sanvito: Eusebius. London, British Museum, *Royal 14. C. 3.* Detail showing B.S.'s italic and roman script.

BARTHOLOMAEVS SANVITVS
CIVIS PATAVINVS ECCLESIAE
S·IVSTINAE MONSILICENSIS
CANONIC·GRATITVDINIS,
ET EXEMPLI AD COLLEGAS
ET POSTEROS ERGO·MANV
SVA IMPENSAQ·CONSCRIPTA
ORNATAQ·EIDEM
D·DEDIT

ANNO DOMINI M·D·IX·

21. Bartolomeo Sanvito: colophon of one of two manuscripts presented to the Collegiate
Church of Santa Giustina in Monselice, signed and dated 1509. Santa Giustina in Monselice

· II ·

IMP · CAESAR VESPA
SIANVS AVG · PONT ·
MAX · TRIB · POTEST · VII ·
IMP · XVII · P · P · CENSOR ·
COS VII · DESIGN · VIII ·

IMP · NERVA CAESAR
AVGVSTVS PONTIFEX
MAXIMVS TRIBVNI
CIA POTESTATE COS ·
III · PATER PATRIAE
REFECIT ·

D

22. Bartolomeo Sanvito: *Silloge* of Fra Giovanni Giocondo (1st recension). Rome, Vatican Library,
Vat. Lat. 10228

IBIDEM·

D·M· FELICI DOMINO FILIO
CARISSIMO FELIX PATER FECIT·

IN HORTIS EIVSDEM·D·ACHILLIS·

L·IVLIO CAELIANO CAELIANA
FILIA PATRI SANCTISSIMO·

IBIDEM·

RVBRIAE TYCHE·T·FLAVIVS HERMES
SODALI OPTIMAE·B·M·F·

Romae in domo·D·Rigeri Archiepiscopi Taranti

DIS · MAN·

C·IVLIO·C·L·
METRODORO
IVLIAE·C·L·
PHAERVSAE
C·IVLIO·C·L·
MERCVRIALIS
VIXIT
AN·XIX·

C·IVLIO·C·F·
METRODORO
VIX·ANN·IIII·
MENS·IIII·
D·XXVI·

C·IVLIO·C·L·
AGATHOPODI
IVLIAE·C·L·
SYMPHERV
SAE

SIBI ET SVIS

POSTERIQVAE AEVORVM·

IBIDEM·

Q·Caecilio Feroci Kalátori·Sacerdótii Titiálium·
Fláuiálium studiófo eloquentiae·Vixit Annis
XV·Menfe·1·Diebus·XXIIII·filio optumo·
ac Reuerentiffimo·M·Gauius Charinus·

23. Bartolomeo Sanvito: *Silloge* of Fra Giovanni Giocondo (3rd recension). The Duke
of Devonshire (Chatsworth)

súp introitu eccé sub duabus figuris.

M ATR. AVG. PIL. EGN. MED.

Ibidem prope.

L. Ateilius. c. f. Stellatina miles praetorianus
cohorte. III.

Lugduni ín vico gurgulionis
in domo Dm Stephani Coloni.

D. m. & memoriae aeternae Arrio attilio honora
to lie inualeriutr morum e nonavior.
rapariorum procurante felicia felicula amica
carissima siue felicius romanus libellicus ponen
dum curauerunt & sub asc. dedicauerunt.

Ibidé in paruo lapide.

F V L G V R   C O N D.

Lugduni ín vico granetarie
ín domo Dm de la roczera.

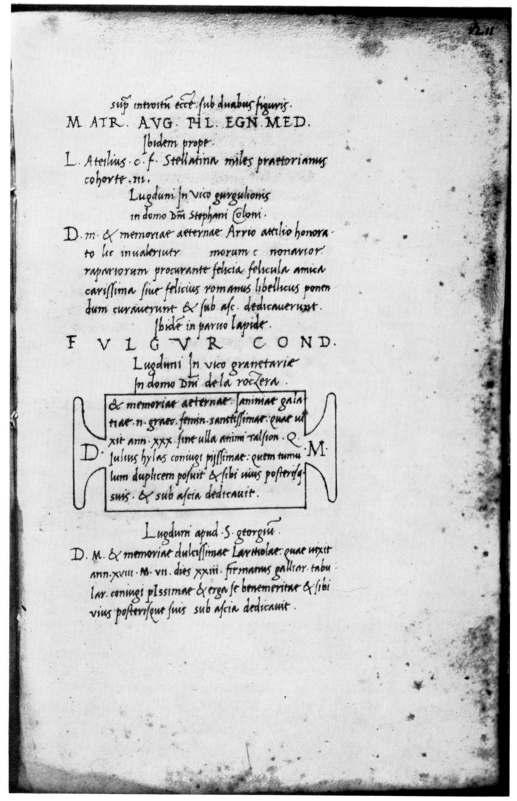

D· & memoriae aeternae animae gaia
tiae. n. graec. femin. sanctissimae quae ui
xit ann. xxx sine ulla animi talsion. Q.
Iulius hylas coniugi piissimae. quem tumu
lum duplicem posuit & sibi uius posterisq;
suis. & sub ascia dedicauit. ·M·

Lugduni apud ·S· georgiu.

D. M. & memoriae dulcissimae Lariuolae· quae uixit
ann. xviii· M· vii· dies xxiii· firmanus galliar. tabu
lar. coniugi pIssimae & erga se benemeritae & sibi
uius posterisque suis sub ascia dedicauit.

24. *Silloge* of Fra Giovanni Giocondo written in various hands, perhaps including Bartolomeo Sanvito.
Venice, Civico Museo Correr, *MS. Cigogna 2704*

emie de . D . Laberio Paeti & Epaphroditi

L . Fausto in monumento C . Luccei Bithi .

L . Fausti Coactoris à portu vinario & . D .

Laberi Paeti . L . Epaphroditi à portu vinario

cum Intro . in monumento eorum eas è regione

osti parietis medi aediculam cum ollis ossuaris

sibi & suis superisque .

In Montesilice agri Patauini Castro in funda

mentis ecclesiae . S . Iustinae sub Trib . figuris .

M . Titi Baelian . Liberti & Famil . Venatoria

Q . Clodio Q . Lib . Fortuito Fil . Q . Clodio Q .

Lib . Nimphio & Clodiae Q . Lib . Primigeniae

amicis Bene merentibus .

IBIDEM .

Maxsuma   T . MAXSVMA TES · FIE · IVS ·

IBIDEM Extra muros Castri .

T . ENNIVS T . F . FAB . SECVNDVS TRIB .

MIL . PRAEF . I . D . CVR . AER . T . F . I .

In Este agri Paduani Castro .   Fra$\overset{cum}{g}$.

L . Mestrius C . F . Rom .   · · · · · · · ·   Leg . IX . · · · ·

IBIDEM ·

ANTONIO VERO SIBI . ET SVIS ·

IBIDEM Ante ecclesiam . S . Martini .

T . Octauio . T . L . Laeto Octauiae . Ɔ . L . Pri

mulae Octauia T . L . Venusta . V . F ·

Epigramma subscripta inuentu fuit apd Este

oppidu supradit tu in agro mei Bartholomei

Sanuiti qui vulgo dicitur Pra in ∨ ase ·

25. Bartolomeo Sanvito: *Silloge* of Fra Giovanni Giocondo (3rd recension). London, British Museum, *Stowe 1016*. Note *in agro mei*

Rome . In . sancta lucia veteri prope Tiberi

VICTORIA VENETIANORVM SEMPER CONSTET
FOELICITER .

Et libella Aegigrammo . Bxi . D. Bartolomei
do : s : vito Coniungimus huius . Et Nittimur Bartholomei fui sui
qui namq3 Et humani . Et magna ipsa intre amo fug

26. Bernardo Bembo, *Zibaldone*: entry referring to Bartolomeo Sanvito. London, British Museum, *Add. MS. 41068*

IVVENALIS VITA
EX ANTIQVORVM
MONVMENTIS·

IVNIVS IVVENALIS

Libertini locupletis incertum alumnus: an filius.
Ad mediam fere ætatem declamauit: animi magis causa: q̃ q̃ scholae aut foro præparar&. Deinde
paucorз uersuum satyra non absurde composita in
Paridem Pantomimum: poetamque: eius semestri-
bus militiolis tumentem: genus scripturæ industrio-
se excoluit. Et tamen bene diu: nē modico quidem
auditorio quicq̃ committere ausus est. Mox magna
frequentia: tantoque successu bis aut ter auditus
est: vt ea quae prima fecerat: infercir& nouis scri-
pturis: Q̃uod non dant proceres dabit histrio. tu
camerinos. Et bareas: tu nobilium magna atria cu-
ras. Praefec tos pelopea facit: philomela Tribunos.
E rat tamen in delicijs aulae histrio. Multique fauto-
rum eius quottidie prouehebantur. Venit ergo ɫ
Iuuenalis in suspitionem quasi Tempora figura-
te notass&: ac statim per honorem militiae q̃uanᷓ
ōt togenarius vrbe summotus est. Missusque ad
Praefec turam cohortis tendentis in extremam
Aegypti partem. Id supplicij genus placuit: vt
leui atque ioculari delic to par esset. Verum
intra breuissimum tempus angore: & tædio perijt.
T emporibus Domitiani floruit: ad Neruae que ɫ

---

27. Bartolomeo Sanvito: Calderini, Commentary on Juvenal. Florence, Biblioteca Laurentiana, *Plut. 53. 2*

41

Cæsari tradiderunt · Atqui cæteris for=
sitan uitio datum ēēt · si se interemissent ·
propterea q̄d eoꝝ uita lenior · & mores
fuerant faciliores · Catoni autem cum in
credibilem tribuissē natura grauitatem:
eamq̄; ipse perpetua constantia robora=
uisset · semperq̄; in proposito susceptoq̄;
consilio permansissē · moriendum potius
q̄ tyranni uultus aspiciendus fuit · Quā
multa passus est Vlysses in illo errore
diuturno : cum & mulieribus (si Circe
& Callypso mulieres appellandæ sunt)
inseruiret · & in omni sermone omnib.
affabilem se ēē uellē · Domi uero & con=
tumelias seruoꝝ ancillaꝝq̄; pertulit · ut
ad id aliquando quod cupiebat peruenи=
ret · At Aiax quo animo traditur mi=
lites oppetere mortem : q̄ illa perpeti ab
alio maluissē · Quæ contemplantes ex
pendere oportebit quid quisq̄; habeat sui
tuiq̄; moderari nec uelle experiri · q̄ se
aliena dedeceant · Id · ɴ · maxime quenq̄;
decē · quod est cuiusq̄; suum maxime ·
S uum igitur quisq̄; noscat ingeniū · acrēq̄;

Catonis grauitas

Vlysses ·
Circe ·
Callypso ·

Aiax

28. Bartolomeo Sanvito: Cicero, *De Officiis*, Rome, 1494. London,
British Museum, *Harl. 6051*

cinora in ciues facere. huc accedebat qᵹ L. Sylla
exercitum : quem in asia due fauerat : quo sibi
fidum faceret / contra morem maiorum luxuri -
ose nimisque liberaliter habuerat. Loca amoe -
na / voluptaria / facile mollierant feroces mi -
litum animos. Ibi prium insueuit exercitus ppli
ro. amare: potare: signa, tabulas pᵉ tas / vasa
caelata mirari. Ea priuatim & publice rapere.
delubra deorum spoliare: sacra profanaquᵉ
omnia polluere. Igitur hi milites, postᵍ uicto -
riam sunt adepti : nihil reliqui uictis fecere. qp -
pe secundae res animos sapientium fatigant:
nedum illi corruptis moribus uictoria tempe -
rarent. Postᵍ diuitia honori esse coeperunt:
& eas gloria imperium potentia sequebantur:
hebescere virtus: paupertas pro probo haberi:
innocentia pro maliuolentia duci coepit. Igitur
ex diuitys iuuentutem / luxuria atquᵉ auaritia
vna cum superbia inuasere: rapere: consume -
re sua: parui pendere: aliena cupere: pudore
pudicitiam: diuina atquᵉ humana promiscua:
nihil pensi: nihilquᵉ moderati habere. operaᵉ

Ex diuitys nascit
superbia &ᵉ ea
tera mala :.

Castaquᵉ beatos paupertate
patres. Iuuenal.

29. Questenberg: manuscript in Rome, Vatican Library, *Ottob. Lat. 2989*

P·VIRGILII MARONIS
BVCOLICA·

AEGLOGA PRIMA·
MELIBOEVS TITYRVS·

ITYRE TV
PATVLAE
RECVBANS
SVB TEGMI
NE FAGI
SILVESTREM
TENVI MVSAM MEDI
TARIS AVENA

Nos patriae fines: & dulcia linquimus arua·
Nos patriam fugimus: tu Tityre lentus i Umbra
Formosa resonare doces Amaryllida siluas·
O Meliboee deus nobis hec ocia fecit
Nanqz erit ille mihi semper deus: illius aram
Sepe tener nostris aboulibus imbuet agnus:

30. Bartolomeo Sanvito (headings, &c.): Virgil. London, British Museum,
Add. MS. 11355

AD TERTIAM VER
EVS
IN AD
IVTO
RIVM
MEVM
INTENDE. R̃. DO
mine ad adiuuandum me
festina. Gl̃ia p̃ri in fine.
Alleluia. HYMNVS.

M Emento salutis auctor:
quod n̄ri &c̃. Antiph.
Maria virgo. PSALMVS.

uo℞ Petri & Pauli: & alio℞
ap̃o℞ nos uere presidiis:
q̃uo℞ domasti fideles esse
doctrinis. ORATIO.

O Mnes sancti tui quesumus
dn̄e nos vbiq̃ adiuuent: vt
dum eo℞ merita recolimus
&c̃. V. in Laudibus: & in fine.
Per dn̄m nostr̄u iesu xp̃m.
&c̃. V. Domine exaudi.
V. Benedicamus dn̄o. ℟.
Deo gr̃as. V. Fideliũ aĩe p̃
misericordiã dei. &c̃.

31. Bartolomeo Sanvito: 'Stewart de Rothesay' Horae. London, British Museum, Add. MS. 20927

32. Matteo Contugi: Petrarch, with *marginalia* by Bartolomeo Sanvito. London, British Museum, *Harl. 3567*

D eterius nrã demetri teq; ugelli
D iscipularum inter iubeo plorare cathedras .
I puer atq; meo citius hec sñscribe libello .
Q Horatij Flacci Sermonu Lib secundus .

Ad Trebatium

S Vnt quibus insatira uidear nimis acer & ultra
L egem tendere opus: sine neruis altera quicquid
C omposui pars esse putat similesq; meorum
M ille die uersus deduci posse trebati
Q uid faciam prescribe faciam quiescas ne inquis
O mnino uersus ʒ operiam male si non
O ptimum erat uerum nequeo dormire ferundi
T ransnanto ubrim somno quibus est opus alto .
I rriguumq; mero sub noctem corpus brito .
A ut si tantus amor scribendi te rapit aude
C esaris inuicti res dicě multa laborum
P remia laturus: cupidum pater optime uires
D eficiunt: neq; enim quis horrentia pilis
A gmina nec fracta pereuntes cuspide gallos .
A ut labentis equo describat uulnera parthi .
A t tamen et iustum poteras et scribě fortem .
S cipiadam ut sapiens lucilus: haud mihi deero
C um res ipa feret: nisi dextro tempore flacci
V erba per attentam non ibunt cesaris aurem .
C ui male si palpare recalcitrat undiq; tutus .
Q uanto rectius hoc q̃ tristi ledě uersu

33. Unknown scribe: Horace, with additions by Bartolomeo Sanvito. London, British
Museum, *Harl. 3510*

Non illum nobis genitrix pulcherrima talem
Promisit graiumq; ideo bis uendicat armis.
Sed fore: qui grauidam imperiis belloq; frementem

LAVS ITALIAE·

Italiam regeret: genus alto a sanguine teucri
Proderet: ac totum sub leges mitteret orbem.
Si nulla accendit tantarᵹ gloria rerᵹ:
Nec super ipse sua molitur laude laborem.
Ascanio ne pater romanas inuidet arces?
Quid struit? aut qua spe inimica gente moratur?
Nec prolem ausoniam? & lauinia respicit arua?
Nauiget hæc summa est. hic nostri nuncius esto.
Dixerat ille patris magni parere parabat
Imperio: & primum pedibus talaria nectit
Aurea: quæ sublimem alis siue æquora supra
Seu terram rapido pariter cum flamine portant.
Tum uirgam capit. hac animas ille euocat orco
Pallenteis: alias sub tartara tristia mittit.
Dat somnos adimitq; & lumina morte resignat.
Illa fretus agit uentos: & turbida tranat
Nubila: iamq; uolans apicem & latera ardua cernit
Atlantis duri: cælum qui uertice fulcit:
Atlanti cinctum assidue: cui nubibus atris
Pinifer caput: & uento pulsatur & hymbri.
Nix humeros infusa tegit: tum flumina mento
Præcipitant senis: glacie riget horrida barba.
Hic primum paribus nitens cyllenius alis
Constitit: hinc toto præceps se corpore ad undas
Misit aui similis quæ circum littora. circum

34. Bartolomeo Sanvito: Virgil, *Aeneid*, showing *antica* script. London, British Museum,
King's 24

A l primo saxo del garzon hebreo .
  Ne cyro in scythia . oue la uedoua orba ,
  Che gran uendetta , e memorabil feo .
C omhuom che sano , en un momento amorba :
  Che sbigottisce , e duolsi colto in acto ,
  Che uergogna con man da gliocchi forba .
C otal era egli . & ancho a peggior pacto :
  Che paura : dolor : uergogna , & ira
  Era nel uolto suo tutti ad un tracto .
N on freme cosil mar quando sadira .
  Ne marine onde , alhor che Typheo piagne :
  Ne mongibel senchelado sospira .
P asso qui cose gloriose e magne
  Chi uidi . e dir non oso a la mia donna
  Vengo . & a laltre sue minor compagne .
E lla hauea in dosso il di candida gonna :
  Lo scudo in man , che mal uide medusa .
  Dun bel diaspro era iui una colonna .

35. Bartolomeo Sanvito: 'Holford' Petrarch, showing *antica* script. Mr. Harvey Frost

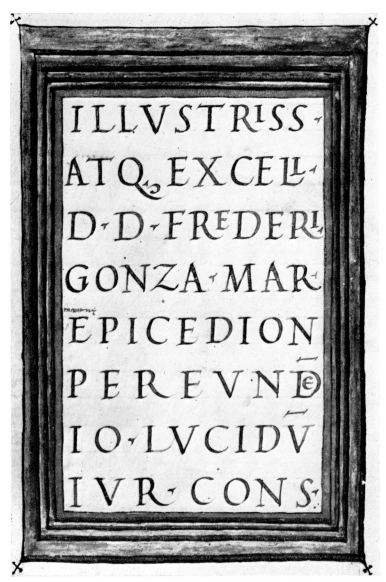

36. Bartolomeo Sanvito: roman capitals written freehand, from manuscript dedicated to Federico Gonzaga (whereabouts not recorded by J. W.)

† Die Januarij 1507·

Li Infrascripti sono li beni & possessione che sono del q. R.do M.r Andriolo de Sancto vito, li quali possedo so Bartheo & de S.to vito q. dñi Aluisy Cane S. Nazarij & Celsi Brixien; Detract la Sexta p.te Introitus dictar possessionu, la qle puiene a M.r Bartheo q. dñi Antony de S.to vito Arciprete de Barbarano.

P°. Una possession posta In la villa de San vito dr Campi Trentanoue p.te aratiui, & p.te pratiui In un pezzo computando el Cortiuo & Casameti; Confina da un lato, uз da Nona la via Comuna; Da Sera M.r vincenzo Grimani; Da null hora I sauri dal ponte de Brenta, & I Lanza dal ponte d brenie, & le Monege d S. Marco pizolo da la banda, & p testa.

I tt Campi quar d terra, li q̃li Confinano co li sop̃ti, excepto chr la via Comuna e In mezo; Et a leuante Confinano le Monege sopdicte; Da nona cioe da una p.te le terre de la chiesa de San vito; Per testa M.r Alouise da cha Longo; Et a sera el dicto M.r Alouise. Se dimandano li sogp̃ti Campi el Terren.

I tt Campi noue ut circa Posti In la Contra di vigri; Confina a nona p testa I Zenari da venesia. A Sera Mad Barbara da cha Barbaro, & el Monast.rio I la Misericordie; A null hora idest de sop p testa Mad B.bara padicta; A doman a longo li frari d li heremitani.

I tt Campo uno ut circa se dimanda el pascolo; Confina d sopra idest a null hora la via Comuna; A matina la Brenta; A nona le Monege d San Marco Pizolo; A sera le terre de la chiesa de San vito.

Item una possession posta In Pra Sotto Este de Campi Quaranexsette ut circa pratiui & aratiui, diuisi In sette p̃te, videlicet Campi xij ut circa, se dimandano le Zenoese; Confinano da doi lati, & da un capo li figlioli del q. M.co M.r Bndetto da Pesaro; Da laltro capo la via Comune.

I tt Campi tre ut circa In la Contrata d li Colombi, Confina da un lato M.r Sebastian Erici; Da un capo la via Comuna; Da laltro la Degora Comuna; Da laltro lato li heredi di Milioni da Este.

I tt Campi Cinque In la Contrata di Preaci, Confina li Zentilhoi da cha da Pesaro sopradicti da doi lati, & da un capo; Da laltro capo la via Consortiua.

I tt Campi diese ut circa In la Contrata de la Longa, Confina da un lato li p̃dti li Zentilhoi da Pesaro; Da laltro I Machiacci de Pra, & Jacomo d Peron, & M.r Antonio de Albrigo hira In Este, & li heredi de Philippo Bressan; Da un capo S Barth° Dulisma da Este; Da laltro la via Consortiua.

I tt Campi Cinq ut circa In la Contrata chiamata d I cinq Campi; Confina da tri lati li Machiacci; Da laltro lato la via Comuna.

37. Bartolomeo Sanvito: inventory of his property. Padua, Museo Civico, *Estimo 1418, Tom. 245, Polizza 53*

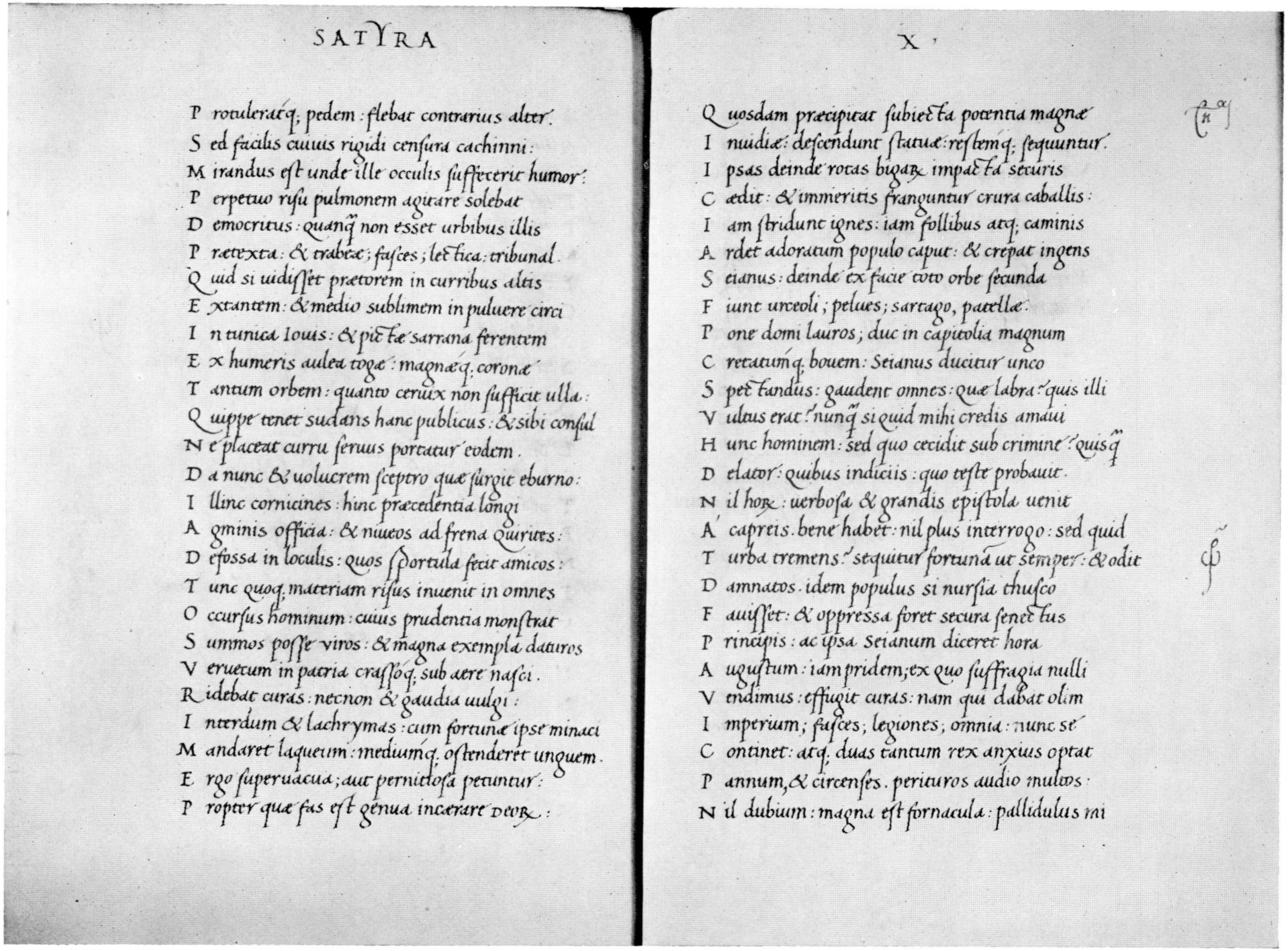

LVCR.

Temporis aeterni quoniam non unius horae
Ambigitur status: in quo sit mortalibus omnis
Aetas post mortem, quae restat cunq; manendo.
Deniq; tantoperce in dubijs trepidare periclis,
Quae mala nos subigit uitae tanta cupido?
Certe equidem finis uitae mortalibus astat:
Nec deuitari letum pote, quin obeamus.
Praeterea uersamur ibidem: atq; insumus usq;
Nec noua uiuendo procaditur ulla uoluptas.
Sed dum abest, quod auemus: id exuperare uidetur
Caetera: post aliud, quod auemus, cum contigit illud: auemus:
Et sitis aequa tenet uitai semper hiantes.
Posteraq; in dubio est, fortunam quam uehat aetas.
Quidue ferat nobis casus: qui ue exitus instet.
Nec prorsum uitam ducendo, deminimus hilum,
Tempore de mortis: nec delibare ualemus,
Quo minus esse diu possimus forte perempti.
Proinde licet quotuis uiuendo condere secla:
Mors aeterna tamen nihilo minus illa manebit:
Nec minus ille diu iam non erit ex hodierno
Lumine, qui finem uitai fecit: & ille
Mensibus, atq; annis qui multis occidit ante.

T. LVCRETII CARI DE RE-
RVM NATVRA LI-
BER IIII

Via pieridum perago loca, nullius
ante
Trita solo: iuuat integros accedere
fontes:
Atq; haurire: iuuatq; nouos decerpe-
re flores:

Insignemq; meo capiti petere inde coronam:
Vnde prius nulli uelarint tempora musae.
Primum, quod magnis doceo de rebus: & artis
Relligionum animum nodis exoluere pergo:
Deinde, quod obscura de re tam lucida pango
Carmina, musaeo contingens cuncta lepore:
Id quoq; enim non ab nulla ratione uidetur.
Nam ueluti pueris absynthia tetra medentes
Cum dare conantur: prius oras pocula circum
Contingunt mellis dulci, flauoq; liquore:
Vt puerorum aetas improuida ludificetur,
Labrorum tenus, interea perpotet amarum,
Absynthi Laticem: deceptaq; non capiatur:
Sed potius tali d tacta recreata ualescat.
Sic ego nunc, quoniam haec ratio plerunq; uidetur
Tristior esse, quibus non est tractata: retroq;
Vulgus abhorret ab hac: uolui tibi suauiloquenti
Carmine pierio rationem exponere nostram:
Et quasi musaeo dulca contingere melle.
Si tibi forte animum tali ratione tenere

cum intra urbem. tum et in agro ad ciuium incolarum
rationes accomodari oportere. proximo superiore
libro disseruimus. Compertumq; fecimus alia cui
um cetui uniuerso alia dignioribus. alia ignobilio
ribus deberi edificia. Quae aut uniuersor grā conuenirent absoluimus.
singulor necessitati Quintus hic liber comodisq; compabitur. Qua in re &
uaria et ampla et difficili explicanda: quoad nobis erit ingenij industrieq;
enitemur. ut intelligas uoluisse me nihil preter mittere. qd aptum ad rem
desiderare quispiam possit. & nihil afferre qd magis ad exornanda ora
tionem q̃ ad exequendum institutum faciet. Ordiendum quide a digni
oribus. Dignissimi omium sunt Quibus rer suma et moderatio comit
tatur. Hi quidem plures erunt. aut vnus. Dignissimũ nimir opot &
esse hunc. qui ceteris presit solus. Quae igit istius unius grā fiat cosede
remus. Sed maximi interest cuiusmodi fore ipm hunc instituamus: il
lius ne similem. qui sancte pieq; impet uolentibus. Quiue nõ magis suis
emolumentis: q̃ suor ciuium salute et cõmodis moueatur. An contra
eiusmodi qui sibi paratam cum sbditis uelit rem. ita ut et inuitis impa;
Nam quom cetera pleraq; omia edificia: tum et urbem ipãm nõ eande
oportet eor ēē quos tyrannos nucupant. atq; eor qui impium quasi
concessum magratum inierint ac tueant. Regum. H. erit urbs mu
nita plus satis: ubi aduenticium arcere hostem ualeat. Tyranno cum sui
nihilo segnius hostes sint q̃ alieni. Vtrinq; munienda ei ciuitas ē aduersus
alienos: aduersusq; suos. & ita munienda ut alienis atq; et suis contra
suos uti sbsidijs ualeat. In hostes urbem supiore libro munita fecimus:
in suos quid expediat consideremus. Peruallidam putat Euripides adu
sariorum multitudinem natura sui. Camq; si fraudem doluq; in unum

40. Pierantonio Sallando: Leonbattista Alberti, *De Architectura*. Rome, Vatican Library, *Vat. Urb. Lat. 264*

Carminibus flaccus: Dedalus ingenio
Gente fluentinus: Marcellus funere: quos
Seruasset lachesis piso futurus erat.
Sed decus hoc raptum / fratres gemineq: sorores
Cum sponsa & patria: luget uterq parens

Gaspar Manius,

Flecte pios oculos hec ad mea uerba uiator
Sic tibi det uitam / qui mihi fata dedit.
Floretina tulit tellus trieteride sexta
Me genitum: & claros ad tulit illa pres.
Lamphredina domus / prenoia certa dederit
Vrsino / lingua cognito utraque bonis.
Flent ciues / mesteq: nurus / miseriq: parentes /
Sed plus una mihi sponsa puella furit.
Virtute prodest (heu) quid coluisse beatam:
Pro meritis mortem / mors inimica dedit.

Bernardinus capella

Quis nisi mestis mops & amari funeris expes
Non misso lachrimis frena relaxat equo?
Tunc cum plaga patet referatis lubrica uenis
flebileq: in medio pectore uulnus hiat

41. Unknown scribe: collection of elegies in memory of Orsino Lanfredini
(died 1488) written in gold on black vellum. London, British Museum,
Add. MS. 22805

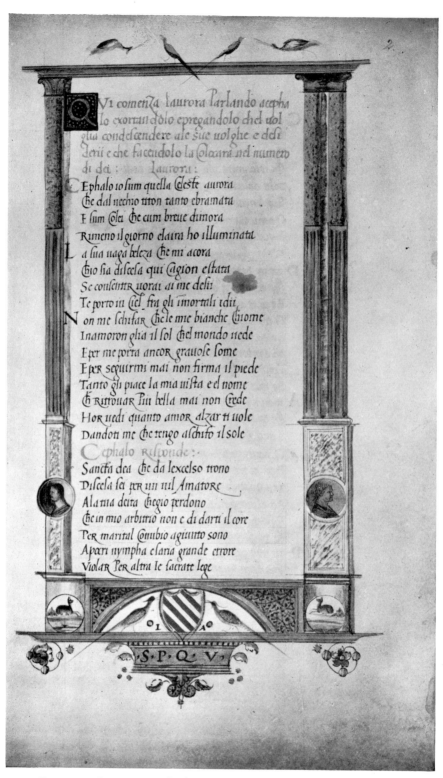

42. Albertus Mapheanus: Niccolò da Correggio, *Cephalo e l'Aurora*. London, British Museum, *Add. MS. 16438*

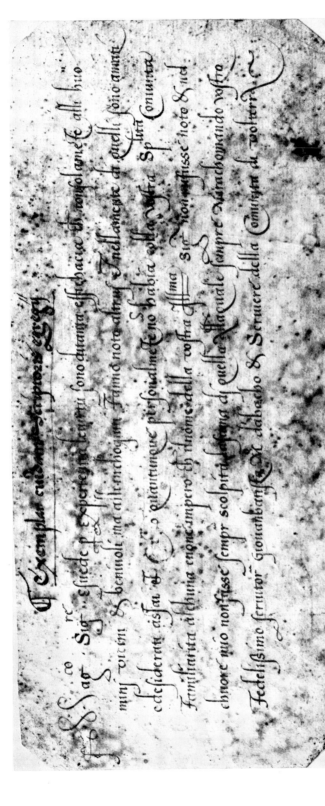

43. Giovanbattista: *Proba*. London, Library of the Brompton Oratory

44. Unknown scribe: Privilege granted to Church of San Giorgio in Alga. Rome, Vatican, *Archivio della Cancelleria della Nunziatura Veneta (Archivio Segreto)*

cialium et iudicum, qui assistant, ac cum nostra, et fratrum Cardinalium præfatorum subscriptione ad bene-placitum officia obtinentium ac ad eorum plenam et sufficientem cautelam gratis ubiꝗ et quandocunꝗ expediri possint. instrumenta quoꝗ et alias obligationes per cameram apostolicam cum clausis et obligationibus uali-dissimis ad sensum officia obtinentium necessariis et oportunis, et quandocunꝗ requisierint et de restituendo eis quicquid exactum solutumue fuisset, nobis ac sedi præfatæ una cum damnis expensis et interesse in omnem euentum inobseruantiæ præmissorum uel alicuius eorum partis fieri et concedi mandamus contrariis non obstantibus quibuscunꝗ. Datum Romæ apud .S. Petrum Die   Mensis   MDXXV Pontificatus Nostri Anno Quarto

Placet et ita Motu proprio facimus . I.

Impressum Romae in Aedibus Ludouici Vicentini
CVM PRIVILEGIO

45. Brief of Clement VII, 1525. Rome, Biblioteca Nazionale, 69. 9. B. 16

S · D · N · CLEMENTI·VII·MEDIC·
PONT · MA~ ·
EVANGELISTA·MAGDALENVS
CAPIFERREVS · FAVSTVS ·
DONVM · DEDIT ·

Vtunc pater lapsis quem
quædam patria nostra dedicis
Carmina Alexandri Iuli
dicimus Leonis:
Et sena Hadriani canti
referenta laudes

Collegissem ad te intenda atqz facenda
Numini mandito totam petervvit sedem
Fama malo Gallos acies uralasq phalanges
Concursisse odiis paribus non viribus aequis:
Retulit et victos iciui ad ulterna gallos
Et geminos capos Reges nutbanq potentum
Exanitam ferro uel aliena compage Vincram
Et eaqrum passim mistum et suic nomne vulgus
Helueuumq fuga morentem in flumnis actu
Nondum tanta dies trepidatu illuxerat orbi

Nox erat extremo in cursu: cum luce futura
Pugnabant tenebræ: vigilabant vtraq, castra.
Igitur columna nouo rutilans atq; ignea nubes
Cæsarianorum supra tentoria uisa est
Gallorumq; oculos radiis perstrinxit et atrum
Cordibus incussit hebetavit luce timorem:
Vox teret de nube tonat clara omnia complens
Fabricius Prosperq, summus da pectora et aures
Nobiscum Deus est o Cæsariane: sequaris:
Lumen imcontinuum lux præuia et unua pandet
Auxilio diuom et montus ruit undiq, miles
In pugnam sequiturq; diem præ nubibus euntis
Illa serenato tenebras fulgore fugabat
Nostrorum ante oculos uiresq; animosq; ministrans
Cæchinnis Fati varijs concipiebus hostes
Tunc Dei hac meliorem pæna militaris obiram
Scis quod pollicitus petitra es uoce Leoni
Felsineum ad Rhenum cui te concordia iunxit
Firma patrum culpaq, tui diciosa Senatus,
Iuraff Isbynas nec adisse tendere ad oras
Et christi socio conquirere marte sepulchrum
Cum tibi ligna crucis gemmato coinidit auro

46. Fausto Capodiferro: verses in his own hand for presentation to Clement VII. Rome, Vatican Library, *Vat. Lat. 10377*

Il Modo

&

Regola de'scriuere' littera
corsiua
ouer Cancellarescha
nouamente' compos to per
Ludovico
Vicenti=
No
Scrittore'de'breui
aplici
in Roma nel Anno di nra
salute'

+ MDXXII +

47. Lodovico Arrighi: *La Operina*. Rome, 1522

uas : alias morales dicimus esse . Liberalitate
autem et temperantiam morales : nam cum de
moribus cuiuspiam loquimur non sapientem il
lum aut sagacem : sed mitem aut temperantem di
cimus esse . Laudamus autem et sapientem ob
habitum . At habituum eos qui laudabiles sunt
uirtutes appellare solemus .

ETHICORVM
ARIST·
LIBRISECVNDI
CAPVT
· I ·

VM AVTEM
Virtus sit duplex : in
tellectiua inquam : atq
moralis . Intellectiua
quidem plurimum ex
doctrina generationem
habet et incrementum . Quapropter experientia
indiget temporeq̃ . Moralis autem assuetudine
comparatur : unde et nomen habuit tale . Ex quo
patet nullam fieri uirtutem morum in nobis na
tura . Nihil enim eorum que sunt natura aliter

48. Lodovico Arrighi: Aristotle, *Ethics*, written in 1517. Amsterdam, University Library, *MS. II. A. 19*

MAGINEM
DOMINI
IESV SALVA
TORIS NOS
TRI

QVAE Singulis quibusqʒ annis ad dimidiatum Augustum a Laterano ad Beatę Mariæ
ad presepe magna pompa circumfertur, priscis quoqʒ temporibus summo apud maiores nostros
in honore' fuisse', tum eius Maiestas que afflictis sepe Po. Ro. rebus opem tulit, tum uetera
monimenta declarant: Nam preterqʒ qʒ Beati Lucę Euangeliste penicillo effictam, noctuqʒ ab
Angelis colores superinductos annales ferant. probatissimi etiam scriptores. maximos et sem
per honores fuisse habitos litteris mandauerunt. Etenim Benedictus Canonicus Basilicę Prin
cipis Apostoloz de Vrbe, Innocenty Secundi familiaris libellum politicum ad Cardinalem
Sancti Marci, is postea Celestinus eius nominis Secundus fuit Circa ANN. ab orbe repa
rato MCXXX. conscribens, in quo omnes cerimonias, supplicationes, adorationesqʒ et quo
ties sacris Pontt. operarentur complexus est, qui adhuc in Sacrario predictę basilicę adser
uatur, Inter cetera hoc quoqʒ quod ad hanc Sacram Imaginem spectare uidetur his uerbis
recenset.

EX LIBRO BENEDICTI CAN·S·P·
N Vigilia Sanctę Marię mane Dñs Papa cum Cardinalibus discalciatis pe
dibus facit. VII. genua, et aperit Imaginem, et deponit uisum cantando Te'
Deum laudamus. Quod constituit LEO QVARTVS PP. In Assū
ptione Sanctę Marię dñs Papa cum omni Curia facit Vesperum et Vigi

49. Lodovico Arrighi: list of benefactors of the hospital of San Giovanni in Laterano. Rome, Archivio di Stato,
MS. 1010

Ill.mo & Excellentiss.o Principi Suoq, p.io & glorioso consilio Humilit. & devote exponit p.io parte sue fidelissi
servitoris & subditi Johannis Antonij de taietis huius originarij Cum sit ch apersuasio de multi virtuosi Zentilhomeni
& tradini El se sia riducto in questa inclita cita p. propallare & insignare El vero Secreto & amaistrameto de
scrivere ogni varietà de litere: ch p homo del modo scrivere si possi Come balla p tuta italia & etia in questa tota
p experientia dal mostrato cū brevita e Bexa poa & deliberado vivere: e morire ne la patria suaz & soto l'om-
bra dela Sublimita Vra dimostrare tale secreto: Ali virtuosi & secretarij dela Vra Signoria: et ad ogni altra p.y
ch di tale virtu, overo Scietra se delectura & Riverentemete Supplica di gra: ch ala Vra Ill.ma Sig.ria piaza
provederli di qualch conveniete Sallario: si ch p. sediante quello el dicto possa vivere Cum la sua famiglia:: Soto
l'umbra di Vra Sublimita: Offerendose Lui de insignare et amaistrare et Scrivere cancellaresco con le sue
rasoni: a tutti li Zoveni dedicati ala cancellaria de Vra ex.tia; S. ne aliqua impensa Ulterius ad ogni altra
p.sona che vora imparare a scrivere soli p. amatori: ō.u. p. ogni sorte de litera ch bel voia: Si Antiqua cancellaresca
mercadantesca. moderna o vero bastarda: & Cuius celsitudini & ōe humilit. Se comedat

50. Giovanantonio Tagliente: supplication to the Doge and the Council of Ten, 1491. Venice, Archivio di Stato, Cons. x, Misti, filza 5, f. 127

La lettera antiqua tonda rechiede grande Z
inggegno di misura, et arte, qual uolen=
do imparar, Prima é neceßario saper far
tutte le letter del sotto scritto Alphabeto

Con ogni soa ragone, et Misura ad una per una, et
cusi imitando ciascun potra facilmente per se farsi ot=
timo scrittore, Et sappi che la legatura della lettera

A. a. b. c. d. e. f. g. h. i. k. l. m. n. o. p. q. r. ſs. t. u. x. y. z.

Tanto uol eser lontana una lettera dallaltra quanto é
larga una gamba dallaltra, essemplo della lettera n.
Et sappi che quella lettera è cancellaresca antiqua
laqual uolendo imparar obserua la R co̅la n̅ra

A. a. b. c. d. e. ff. g. h. i. k. l. ll. m. n. o. p. q. r. s. t. u.
x. y. z.

51. Two pages from Tagliente, writing book, Venice, 1524

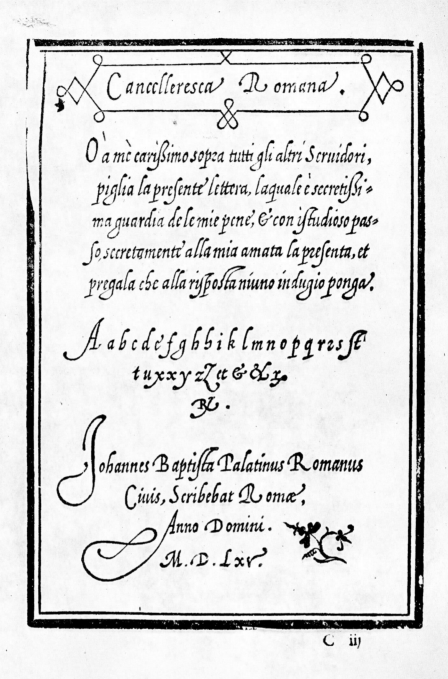

Cancelleresca Romana.

O a mè carissimo sopra tutti gli altri Seruidori,
piglia la presente lettera, laquale è secretissi=
ma guardia de le mie pene, & con istudioso pas=
so, secretamente alla mia amata la presenta, et
pregala che alla risposta niuno indugio ponga.

A a b c d e f g h h i k l m n o p q r s s ſ
t u x x y z z tt & & ſ y
z .

Johannes Baptista Palatinus Romanus
Ciuis, Scribebat Romæ,
Anno Domini.
M. D. Lxv.

52. Giovanbattista Palatino: *Compendio del gran volume.* Rome, 1566

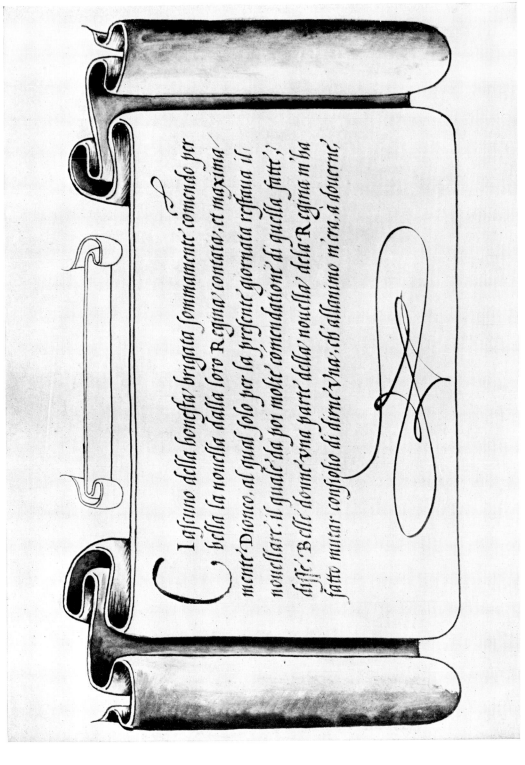

Lasiuno della honesta brigata sommamente comendo per bella la nouella dalla loro Regina contata, et maxima mente Dioneo, al qual solo per la presente giornata restaua il nouellare, il quale da poi molte comendationi di quella fatte, disse, Belle donne vna parte della nouella della Regina m'ha fatto mutar consiglio di dirne vna, ch'all'animo m'era, a douerne'

53. Giovanbattista Palatino: *cancellaresca* from a manuscript in the Bodleian Library, Oxford, *Canon. Ital. 196*

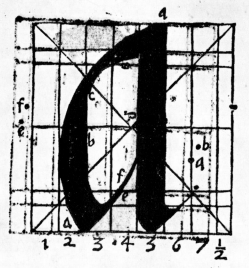

LA lettera .A. si forma nel suo quadro il qual tu partirai come io t'ho detto : & per far il suo caso metterai il compasso nel punto del .a. che sta nella 7. linea sotto il diametro, & risponda sopra la .6. linea doue ti segna un'altra .a. & farai mezo circolo che fornisca alla .3. linea doue trouarai un'altra .a. Il suo ouato, ouer cauo si forma in tre mezi circoli, cioè mettendo il compasso nel punto del .b. che trouarai alla .7. linea sotto il diametro, & risponda alla .3. linea, & cominciarai dal detto diametro doue ti segna l'altro .b. & uenirà al mezo della terza testa: il secondo sarà il punto del .c. il qual trouarai nella linea che serra il quadro à mano manca sopra il diametro, & risponderà il compasso alla .3. linea cominciando dal detto diametro, et andarà di sopra fin alla linea angolare: il terzo sarà il punto del .d. il qual trouarai nella .5. linea sopra il diametro, & risponda di sopra la medesima linea, & alla prima linea sotto quella del quadro, & uenirà fin alla angolare, che si leghe con quella del .c. La sua tondezza di sotto si forma mettendo il compasso nel punto del e, & risponda sotto la .3. linea, & farai mezo circolo che arriui alla .5. linea sotto il diametro, farai unaltro mezo circolo sopra questo, & discosto un quinto mettendo il com.passo nel punto del .f. liquali due punti .e, & .f. trouarai a man dritta di fuora al quadro, & sarà formato il caso. La sua gamba uuole esser dritta, et discosta dal detto caso due teste. In loco di base farai una testina sguinza conforme a i punti che trouarai. E te bisogna auuertire che come hai fatto questa .a. farai il b.c.d.e.

g.h.o.p.q.x. con quelli medesimi punti, et circoli. Et questo ti basti hauendo l'essemplare inanzi.

LA lettera .B. si forma come l'a, saluo chel suo astillo esce fuora del quadro tre teste, & meza, & della prima testa sopra il quadro farai la sua tondezza con un poco di testina anchora in tondo: & per farla seguirai l'ordine de i punti come nell'a. & questo astillo ti seruirà per d.f.h.l.

54. Ferdinando Ruano: *Sette Alphabeti* Rome, 1554

INCIPIVNT EPISTOLAE DOMINI HILDEBERTI
PRIVS CENOMANNENSIS EPISCOPI
POSTEA TVRONEN ARCHIEPI.
INCIPIT EPISTOLA. D

Onuersione et conuersatione tua letatur et exultat
anima mea, illum prosequens actione gratiarum, cu
ius est, quod nunc tandem philosophari decreueris,
Nondum quippe redolebas philosophum, cum exac
quisita philosophorum scientia morum tibi minime depromeres ve
nustatem. Nunc autem sicut ex fauo mellis dulcedinem, sic ex ea
bene agendi formulam expressisti. Hinc est quod ecclesiasticis digni
tatibus omissis, elegisti abiectus esse in domo Dei, magis quam habi
tare in tabernaculis peccatorum. Hinc est quod ambitiosam suppelle
ctilem in exorabili odio persequeris, quod institoriam abdicas lectione,
quod magnum questum iudicas, pietatem cum sufficientia. Hinc deniq
est, quod intra fines virtutis totum te colligis, quod de vita tua cum na
tura deliberas, minus attendens quid caro possit, quam quid spiritus
vellit. Hoc vere philosophari est. Sic viuere, magnum iam cum supe
ris est inire consortium. Nulla hinc ad coelos via compendiosior. Eo
facile peruenies, si tamen exoneratus incesseris. Porro animus ipse
tibi sarcina est, donec et sperare desinat et timere. Nondum enim bea
te viuit, quem vel voti torquet dilatio, vel a uoto decidendi metus excru
ciat. Diogenes quia nullius sperauit fauorem, nullius potentiam for
midauit. Ille in dolio suo tam spe vacuus quam timoris expers, locu
pletem transegit paupertatem. Porro quae sic infidelis cynicus abhor

IVLIVS   PONT.
  III   MX

55. Ferdinando Ruano: Hildibertus, Epistolae, opening page. Rome, Vatican Library, *Vat. Lat. 3841*

A a b c d ə e c f f g g h h k l M m n o p q x

Finalmente si comprendeno gli intrinsichi pensieri degli huomini confabulando seco, dalli cottidiani ragionamenti, dalli loro movimenti et da altre mille sopravenienti occasioni. Onde gli sapientissimi, et esperimentantissimi Philosophi insegnorono alla posterità de questi documenti, per il che obligatissimi sempre dobbiamo tenere alle memorie loro imitando con ogni nostro studio et diligentia vigilantissimamente, quanto quelli s'affaticorono felice, a nostro beneficio, ornamento et perpetua verità, et così fuggiremo ogni nota d'ingratitudine che si attribuisse all'oblivio.

p q r s t u u r y z z delsare

& B p̄ p̄ p̄ g

56. Vespasiano Amphiareo or Albertacci: manual. Venice, 1554

La virtù è aguisa che mai non si perde, fiume che non si passa,
mare che non si nauiga, fuoco che mai si ammorza, tesoro che mai
si finisce, essercito che mai si vince, caualo che mai si posa, sfida che
sempre torna, guardia che non s'inganna, camino che non si sente,
et fama che mai perisce. O figliuolo se sapessi che cosa è essere da bene, et quanto saresti da bene essendo virtuoso, à Iddio saresti ser-
uigio, à te' daresti buona fama ne' tuoi poneresti piacere, ne forastieri
genereresti amore, et tutto il mondo ti amerebbe, et temerebbe

Ioannes Franc̃ Crescius Romæ Scribebat

57. Gianfrancesco Cresci: *Essemplare*, Rome, 1560

Ill.mo et R.mo Monsig. et pad.ne mio Oss.mo

Hauendo inteso molti giorni sono da M. Giouan'Luigi, (q'lmente) V. S. Ill.ma ha riceu-
ute le mie lettere scrittele, sotto li. 4. et xvj di giugno passato, le q'l'erano di
un medes.mo tenore, sono restato tuttauia maggiormente consolato, intendendo la
continua protettione, che qlla ha tenuto fin hora per me, contro di coloro, che
sollecitauono di balzar M. Giouan'luigi dal mio loco della libraria, della qle
cosa l'obbligo grande, che gliene sento, lo potrà meglio giudicar lei, che io
per hora esplicargliene. Hora ql che mi occorre dirlo con q'sta mia,
è ch'essendo stato uenti anni passati in Roma, lontano da mio padre, et
ritrouandosi lui molto uecchio, et non hauendo altri figlioli, che me, che lo
aiutti, et n'habbi cura, et massime quando gli accade indisposit.ne, mi pare
molto strano ad absentarm. da lui, et non li tener quella debita compag.a, che à
me conuiene per quel poco tempo, che gli resta di uita, massime essendo, che
per la sua uecchiezza potrebbe facilmente mancare di q'sta uita, et l'absentia
mia causarli à lui, et à me maggior trauaglio, oltre che io particolarm.te
ne harei anco molto danno, p non hauer persona che confidar mi potessi, et
che tenesse il conto delle cose mie qui in Milano. Et questo fra l'altre
fu la principal causa della mia partita di Roma et che io lasciasse

58. Gianfrancesco Cresci: letter to Cardinal Sirleto, 1572. Rome, Vatican Library, *Vat. Lat. 6185*